Maureen

may the Great Life
guide you
to fill your 'boots'
and become

Being Human.

Alicia Ray

Solicitor

Being Human

Being Human

Exploring the Forces that Shape us and Awaken an Inner Life

**Solihin and Alicia Thom
and Alexandra ter Horst**

Ad Humanitas Press - Portland

First printing 2004
Second printing 2005
Third printing 2006
Fourth printing 2008
Copyright © 2004 – 2008 by Solihin and Alicia Thom and Alexandra ter Horst

Published by Ad Humanitas Press

3105 SE Clinton Street
Portland, OR 97202 United States of America

Permissions appear on page 155
All verse without attribution is written by the authors.

Publishers Cataloging-in-Publication Data
(Provided by Quality Books, Inc.)

Thom, Solihin.
    Being Human : exploring the forces that shape us and awaken an inner life / Solihin and Alicia Thom, and Alexandra ter Horst.
        p. cm
        ISBN 0-9713172-0-8

    1. Self-actualization (Psychology) 2. Spirituality.
    3. Interpersonal relations. 4. Spiritual life.
    5. Humanity. 6. Consciousness. 1. Title

    BF637.S4T46 2004   158.1
                    QBI03-700565

Cover painting: *Being Human*, and other illustrations by Lachlan Thom
Cover design: Lachlan Thom
Art Direction: Martina Klimova
Authors' note: we have chosen to use a plural subject with a singular verb (for example, "our animal self") to maintain our connection to the reader without losing the meaning of the information presented

This 2008 edition printed in the United States of America

08 07 06 05 04   5 4 3 2 1

To our parents who gave us life
William and Diana Thom
Lambert and Maria Gibbs
Fredrick and Margaret Rodgers
and our children
Sofiah, Lachlan, Rebecca, and Miriam
and
Jonathan, Martha, and Jerald
whose presence in our lives
brings a depth and richness that is immeasurable

Being Human

Acknowledgements

We wish to acknowledge with deepest gratitude Muhammad Subuh Sumohadiwidjojo (1901–1987), founder of the spiritual association of Subud, who brought us the latihan and introduced us to the life forces.

Also our colleague and friend Francois Reynolds who, with Solihin, in the early days shaped the initial foundation of this work, and with whom we facilitated our first Life Forces workshops.

We also greatly appreciate the efforts of the following people who read our draft copy and whose comments were instrumental in shaping the final version of this book: Alexandra Asseily, Deborah Auslander, Pamela Burry-Trice, Reynold Feldman, Karen Kernan, Adriana King-Hall, Andrew Linial, Janet March, Francois Reynolds, Sasha Robertshaw, Margaret Rodgers, Harris Smart, Anita Soos, Jerald ter Horst, Allison Shadday, Sofiah Thom, Garrett Thompson, James Toffolo, David Week, and our editor Linda Gray. Thanks to Markus Blocher, Tomas Jones, Beata Moreno, Maurice Palfreyman, and Judy Wise for sharing their stories with us.

Finally, our sincere thanks and deepest appreciation to Peter ter Horst and all of our children for their unwavering support of the three of us during the creation of this book.

Being Human

Contents

Being Human

I am the earth

yet I can arise from it

I am the trees and flowers

yet I can expand far beyond them

I am the animals who roam the earth

yet I can soar high above them

I am all of humanity

yet a servant only to the One

I know who I am

Introduction

Apart from the physical characteristics that give us our human appearance, the music, art, and culture that inspire our human feelings, and the moral and ethical ideologies that govern our human actions, all humans possess another remarkable and unique quality: the need to truly know ourselves and our purpose in life.

Most of us assume that we are human because we inhabit a human body. But there is a difference between our *form* as humans and our *content*. Just as the human body represents the form of who we are, our inner self represents our content. This inner self exists inside every human. By exploring the forces that shape us and our relationship with them, we will begin to understand what it means to truly come alive and awaken an inner life.

Each of us has the capacity to lead both an inner and outer life. Our outer lives are what most of us would think of as the "doing" part of us. These include our daily routines of work and play, our interactions with others, and the fulfillment of our material needs. Our inner lives represent the "being" part of us—the essence of who we are, our true Self, and our connection to the Divine. When these two parts are harmonious they become one, so that our outer actions, thoughts, and feelings are guided by our inner Self.

Many of us are unfamiliar with or unaware of the concept of an inner life because we tend to allow the demands of our outer lives to take precedence. We live in a world whose accelerated pace is driven by technology and the attempt to appease our insatiable appetite for that which is more, bigger, or better. We live frenetic lives in order to meet our practical needs for food, income, and a roof over our heads. We may long to live simpler, less complicated lives, but the force of our culture makes this challenging. Thus, we fall into a collective consciousness, running here and there, hustling to acquire the next dollar, the next possession. When external forces take power over us we allow them to dictate our choices. When we forget our connection to the Divine and fail to acknowledge this unseen hand in our daily lives, we are left hungry for some deeper meaning. Thus, the integration of an inner and outer life is essential. Although we may wish for more balance in our lives, we often put off or defer doing something about it until we are confronted with an illness or crisis that forces us to stop and reassess our priorities.

Historically, people viewed the world as being primarily material—composed of the seen and the rational, yet governed by other elements, largely unseen, that exerted a force. The need to explain the unseen is a common thread that runs throughout all cultures. One way that people explained the actions of these forces was through the use of story. It was the role of the storyteller to pass along the wisdom of the past through lore and the fine art of telling a tale. These stories told of characters' vagaries, proclivities, and weaknesses, yet also illustrated the ultimate strength, morality, patience, and nobility of those very same people as they faced the challenges of their journey.

Throughout the ages, fairy tales, fables, mythologies and other types of stories have been used to impart knowledge of the odyssey of humankind by touching upon some unconscious aspect of the inner self. Although these stories are often set in other times and places, they have a universal relevance to us in our own time and to our own lives. They convey an understanding implicit in the collective human consciousness. These archetypal stories exist to teach us about the forces and elements that we all encounter in ordinary life. Archetypal forms or symbols are everywhere, and our ability to recognize and interpret them is inherent in our genetic coding. Although embedded within time-honored interpretations and ideas, archetypes can also awaken within us the promise of something new.

Exploration of the life forces has been the foundation of our workshops for more than fifteen years, during which time we have received many requests to write a book about our understanding and experiences. The intent of this book is not only to explain in everyday language something that we, and others, have found invaluable, but also to highlight the importance of living a life in which a union exists between our inner and outer selves. This is the essence of being human.

We recognize that many people whose perspectives are quite different from our own will read this book. An individual's view of the world is shaped by

One of our workshop participants illustrated this idea when she introduced herself by saying that she had received a tremendous gift—cancer. She then explained that this had compelled her to make the changes that would support both her inner and outer life.

Odyssey: An adventurous journey marked by many changes of fortune.

Truth, naked and cold, had been turned away from every door in the village. Her nakedness frightened the people. When Parable found her she was huddled in a corner, shivering and hungry. There, she dressed Truth in story, warmed her and sent her out again. Clothed in story, Truth knocked again at the villagers' doors and was readily welcomed into the peoples' houses. They invited her to eat at their table and warm herself by their fire.

—Jewish teaching story

their background of spiritual and religious beliefs and life experiences. Some of us may be separated from our faith or uncertain about our beliefs. Others will have adopted a new approach. It is not our intent to convey that one must embrace a particular spiritual path or belief in order to benefit from this book. We therefore acknowledge that our references to God, the Great Life, the Source, the Divine, the Creator, and the One are simply our way of naming that which is greater than ourselves.

We invite you to join us on a journey that can lead to a wider and deeper understanding of the forces that shape your life. You will begin to recognize your own unique ontology—the sequence of events that has brought you to your present state. Interpreting these events in the context of the life forces can help you unravel the mystery of why you say one thing and do another, get stuck in a rut, become swamped by your feelings, or adhere to ideas and beliefs that are limiting. Understanding how these forces operate within you creates the possibility of real and lasting change.

We suggest that as you read this book you take time to reflect on how its contents relate to your own life. It is our hope that you find it relevant in a deeply personal and experiential way.

Solihin and Alicia Thom • Portland, Oregon
Alexandra ter Horst • Asheville, North Carolina
October, 2003

1

A Human Map

We shall not cease from exploration
and the end of all our exploring
will be to arrive where we started and
know the place for the first time.

—T.S.Eliot

R ecently, Alicia and I were invited to attend a peace conference in Kalimantan, the Indonesian part of the island of Borneo. Prior to the beginning of the conference, we traveled upriver by boat, eventually diverting off on a smaller tributary to visit a remote village. We wandered through the jungle community of the Dyaks, the indigenous people of the interior of the island. As dusk approached we were invited into a home, where we were served arak, a delicious palm wine with a soft, velvety taste that belies its potency. As we sipped our drinks, I couldn't help but notice that a baby girl seated across from me had a terrible squint in one of her eyes. Through Alicia, who translated, I explained my background as a physician and asked if I might have a look at her. Her grandfather, in whose arms she was nestled, readily agreed. Using my therapeutic protocol, I placed my hands upon her head and waited for the tissues causing this condition to release of their own accord. Half an hour later the tissues complied, and she was happily returned to her grandfather, her eye appearing much better.

Our human map is the means by which we understand and make sense of our life.

We were then told that her grandfather had himself been in a moribund state for the past eighteen months. I looked at him, a small man with a wispy moustache, and noticed that his entire demeanor illustrated a loss of will. I asked if he would like me to work with him, and he nodded. As I worked with him, I discovered that eighteen months prior he had unexpectedly lost both his brother and cousin. Their deaths had, in a way, enshrouded him, and he had allowed the feeling of death to fully penetrate his consciousness. I wondered how I could explain this dynamic in terms that these people could understand. I was pleasantly surprised after Alicia relayed the information to the man and his friends. Not only did they wholeheartedly agree with my explanation, they accepted it as if it were a normal, everyday topic. I realized then that, despite the obvious differences between us, we were able to share a common perspective.—Solihin

Our human genome has evolved and developed over millions of years. We know that we receive half of our genetic instructions—our genetic blueprint—from our mother and half from our father. What is less widely recognized is that, although our individual blueprint is unique (except in identical twins and the occasional multiple birth), 99.9 percent of the DNA contained in human beings is identical, indicating that we have a common human blueprint. Unfortunately, this commonality is often obscured when the emphasis is placed on the differences between "us" and "them." We then become separate from those we perceive as "the other." Conversely, if we embrace those differences we can enrich our human experience, giving us the feeling of being a part of the whole of humankind.

Implicit in most spiritual heritages is the recognition that we all originate from a primary Source, to which each of us longs deeply to return. The great poet and philosopher Kahlil Gibran alluded to this when he spoke of "life's longing for itself." This adds a new dimension to the human blueprint. Unlike our genetic instructions, however, it is not composed of strands of DNA passed on through our lineage, nor can its contents be examined under even the most powerful microscope. Instead, it originates from the Divine, and it contains the inner instructions that support and guide each of us on our journey through life. This Divine blueprint defines the essence of who we are, and provides the impetus to find our true purpose and realize our potential. It inspires in us a sense of awe and wonder about life itself and compels us to deepen our connection to the Source.

During our lifetime, our human blueprint is shaped and modified, creating our own unique map. It is colored by our culture, religion, beliefs, gender, genetic coding, and life experiences, all of which act as filters through which we see the world. As we navigate the journey of our life, this map governs our feelings, actions, thoughts, and ultimately how we align ourselves to a central or guiding principle. We are sometimes surprised to learn that our own map is not the same as everyone else's. Because we are limited to our own perspective—our own map—each of us interprets what we see differently. It is therefore important to remember that "the map is not the territory."

Our family of origin and the environment in which we grow up influence how we set the direction of our "compass" to locate and discern our pathway through life.

Growing up in England with British versions of the world map, I always saw Britain and Europe as being in the center of the map, with North and South America off to the left and Russia and Asia off on the right. One day someone mentioned the relatively close proximity of Japan to the west coast of America, and I was confused. My childhood years of picturing Japan on the opposite side of the map had made it seem far away. It was not until I looked at a globe that I got things in perspective!

When I saw an American version of a world map for the first time, it provided a very different view—the Americas were right in the middle! It made me realize how differently we see things because of where we are standing, whether it is in Asia, Africa, America, Europe, or India. Our different reference points affect our perspectives.—Alicia

After a medieval cartographer had drawn upon all of his geographical knowledge in the making of a map, he would neatly letter in the space beyond, "Here Be Dragons." It is interesting how we continue to view that which is beyond the known as dangerous or threatening!

Life gives us the opportunity to expand or redraw our own map, which provides a broader perspective and width of consciousness. But some of us do not wish to venture into uncharted areas, even when we acknowledge that they exist. Instead, we remain content with what is known and familiar. Others may be willing to explore the far corners of their maps, perhaps encountering ill-defined areas that are largely unknown. The most adventurous will go to the edge and be prepared to stretch their boundaries in search of an extension of their old worldviews.

The differing reactions to the events of September 11, 2001 illustrate how different responses are generated by different maps. For some, the issue was black and white—the United States had no choice but to retaliate. For others, the overwhelming feeling of fear left them paralyzed and held in emotional limbo. Some people viewed the unprecedented attack on mainland America as a call to arms to defend our territory. Others felt compelled to protest against military action, determined to respond in a more peaceful and humanitarian manner. Many tried to understand the complex issues that precipitated these events, and as a result broadened their perspective.

The three of us were working together in Portland, Oregon on September 11. We had no television and did not receive news of the attacks until Peter, Alexandra's husband, phoned from Los Angeles.

As we turned on the radio and heard the poignant, horrific unfolding of the drama, I found myself oddly unmoved. I felt an internal stillness and

a feeling that this was much bigger than the tragedy and inhumanness of the immediate events. Of course, over the following three or four days, as we listened to the continuous NPR broadcasts and watched the grainy broadband videos on our computer, the empathy, sadness, and pathos we witnessed made me move from a place of inner quietness into my emotions. As a Muslim, I felt tremendous sorrow at the thought of how misunderstood Islam would be as a result of this terrorist action. Nowhere in the Qu'ran (the holy book of Islam) does it infer that such an action is justifiable, and indeed, the Qu'ran always tempers any warlike or defensive posture with the idea that peace is always preferable, and that the killing of innocents is completely against God's wishes.

After witnessing the events that have panned out since then, I still feel that this event was pivotal, a global shift, an unveiling of human dynamics largely unspoken, unreported, and misunderstood. This toppling of an ivory tower, a symbol of materialism, may prompt, in the long run, another long, hard look at the politics of consumption, the pursuit of a dream. Perhaps this will move us towards a globalization based upon a human ethos rather than one that satisfies material needs. The truth is that the black and the white of any matter is never static. It is interchangeable. Within one is the other, as the Taoist symbol of yin and yang clearly illustrates. In the darkness is the light—in the light is the darkness. It is within the grasp of all of us to challenge and meet these aspects within ourselves, so that we can understand why others might pick up the gun, light the fuse, or give up their life for their cause.—Solihin

Deeply shocked and saddened by the intensity of what had happened, I had a sense that this action had initiated a major change in the world that day, and particularly, of course, in America. It felt as though so much had changed almost anything seemed possible. I had the sense that we had been presented with an enormous opportunity, if we chose to take it, to look beneath the surface and ask ourselves, and each other, the difficult questions that needed to be asked—to try and understand the sequence of events that had led to this horrendous action. I felt great hope that this could be the beginning of a change in the world, that we might look beyond our own and see ourselves as an integral part of the world community. I wondered if this was the first time in the history of the world that so many had been united in prayer and sentiment. I felt that here was a chance for America to show its humanity by responding in a way that was new, unexpected, and unprecedented. I still feel that in these troubled times we have been given an opportunity for transformation, but we need to take it. We each need to recognize the importance of being willing to understand and know each other; of discovering what unites us, rather than what divides us; of finding a common vision and purpose wider and deeper than our own personal or national needs. Here lies the chance for us all to live our humanity.—Alicia

When Peter called from Los Angeles that morning, I answered the phone. His voice was strained and shaky in a way that I had never before heard. "Have you seen the news?" he asked. His call came moments after the second tower had been struck, and as he relayed the events of the early morning hours to me, I felt a part of myself saying, "this is not real, it cannot possibly be real." I walked into the kitchen where Solihin and Alicia were making breakfast, as yet unaware of what had happened. I remember bracing the countertop with my hands, my voice faltering as I tried to explain to them what Peter had just told me.

In the days that followed, I experienced a wide range of emotions. As an American, I immediately felt the pain and violation of the first-ever attack on our mainland. My initial reaction on that day was a strong feeling that we should somehow retaliate for what, to me, amounted to nothing more than calculated, cold-blooded murder. Yet seeing the outpouring of love and sympathy for our country and feeling the quiet "hush" that seemed to envelop the world in the hours and days that followed was tremendously comforting to me. As time passed, I recognized a part of me that, more than anything else, longed to live in a peaceable world. I started to wonder if retaliation would really be to anyone's benefit, or if, in fact, it would only generate more animosity toward Americans and inevitably spawn more acts of violence against innocent people. For the first time in my life I wanted and needed to understand why someone hated Americans enough to orchestrate an event of such proportion. It would be the beginning of a process that continues within me even now as we enter into another conflict in the Middle East. The answers I seek are not simple, are not in any book, and have not been born out by history. They are not about the rights and wrongs of our president, our countrymen, or the American military men and women pursuing liberty and justice for all. The answers I seek are only about me, about how I feel and act and what I believe about others who also call this planet their home. I think Pablo Casals summed it up beautifully when he said, "The love of one's country is a splendid thing. But why should love stop at the border?"—Alexandra

The human map is complex and multidimensional, and it shifts and develops as we face the challenges of life. Something unexpected might force us to question our feelings, the motives behind our actions, or the reasons for our strong beliefs. The result is that we expand or in some way redraw our map. This begins the development of human consciousness. Life changes as a consequence.

2

The Life Forces

I died as a mineral and became a plant,
I died as a plant and turned to animal.
I died as animal and became man,
what fear I then, as I cannot diminish by dying?

—Jelaluddin Rumi

For thousands of years, humans have attempted to make sense of and understand their relationship with the earth, plant, animal, and human realms as well the wider universe. Their traditions and rituals have formed the foundation for worship, given order to life, and provided the means to sustain these beliefs over time. Ancient pagan religions embraced a geocentric view of the world and attributed magical qualities to the natural realms. Tribes used dance and ritual to appease the natural and supernatural elements of the earth, and they designated a chosen few within the community to manipulate these forces through ceremony and knowledge. These ancient models of spirituality were the first attempts to make sense of the Divine; different versions of these models existed in every culture.

In eastern cultures the shamanic ideas of northern Mongolia were combined with the philosophy of Buddhism to form Taoism. This brought the elements of suffering, service, and the manipulation of the forces into an organized, principled, and erudite human philosophy. In Taoism, humankind was seen as the balancing intermediary in the interplay between the forces of earth, our own elements, and those of the heavens. Hinduism, on the other hand, saw the extraordinary handiwork of the Creator in the single deity of Brahma, yet Hindus essentially created a polytheism through which they worshipped all aspects of the Creator. The underlying structures of all human beliefs, whether pagan, polytheistic, or monotheistic, all acknowledge the interplay between human beings and the forces outside them.

Early monotheistic doctrines explained man's existence in terms of a hierarchy. Around 250 A.D., the classic philosopher Plotinus spoke of the One, or Absolute, from which emanated Intelligence, from which emanated Soul, from which emanated Matter. Plotinus rejected materialism in his search for ecstatic union with the Divine. From his ideas arose the Neoplatonic view that living in the material world can cause us to forget the purpose of our existence: reunion with the Divine. This philosophy has strongly influenced monotheistic religious thought.

In Judaic mysticism, the Kabbalah emerged from the conceptualization of existence as ten emanations, or aspects, of Creation. It suggests that from the Absolute came God the father, and from there the other subordinate levels developed.
These subordinate kingdoms included the angelic worlds and those of matter,
—the celestial bodies and those of our world.

In Islam, these ideas were furthered through the work of Sufi philosophers
and later became part of Muslim understanding in relation to the hierarchy of
the elements within us. This hierarchy consisted of the lower selves (*nafs*) and
the higher elements or spirit (*ruh*), which were recognized as having an influence on the human. Muslims believed that perfection was attained through
the mastering of the lower selves and the cultivation of the higher elements
within us, and they recognized the human as the intermediary between Allah
(God) and the earth.

The idea of a hierarchy is central to what are known as the life forces. A *force* is
the power, strength, or energy that initiates a change of state. When Einstein
spoke of energy as matter in motion, he referred to the movement of particles
at a subatomic level. Because this movement is invisible to the naked eye, we
might assume that all matter contains only latent or potential energy. In fact,
this energy is present at all times, which implies that all matter *is* energy. All
energy contains a particular frequency, or waveform, and each of the kingdoms—material, vegetative, animal, and human—has a specific carrier wave.
Each of these carrier waves represents a force.

Nothing happens until something moves.

—Albert Einstein

Just as our external world is composed of material, vegetative, animal, and human forces, we, too, are composed of, influenced, and supported by these same
elements. We call these the *life forces*, and they are present both within us and
in the world around us. We can illustrate and differentiate them as a hierarchy,
beginning with the material force and moving upwards through the vegetative,
animal, human and noble levels towards the Divine—the primary life force
from which all other forces originate.

Our own introduction to the life forces came from Muhammad Subuh Sumohadiwidjojo, the founder of the spiritual association of Subud, of which we
are longtime members. He spoke of and explained his understanding of the

life forces in the language of Islamic theology and Javanese mysticism, which has its roots in Hinduism. By interpreting our own life experiences in the context of the life forces, coupled with our surrender to God, our personal understanding of them began to develop.

Various systems of theology use different nomenclature and descriptions to illustrate what we refer to as the life forces. Our challenge in this book is to elucidate historical and contemporary theological understanding without using language that is arcane or difficult to grasp. Some emanation theories suggest seven, nine, or even ten levels or spheres of influence, the highest of which are beyond the comprehension of most of us. These higher forces fill and animate those who are known as saints, prophets, and holy men and women. For this reason, we will instead focus on the five forces that we all encounter and that directly affect our lives.

The development of a human embryo closely parallels the first four levels of the life forces hierarchy. It sequentially layers and displays the genetic blueprint (the material life force), animates the physiological systems and organs (the vegetative life force), develops gender, functional mobility, and survival characteristics (the animal life force), and finally culminates in the maturation of the neocortex (the human life force) as the fetus differentiates and develops as a human creature.

We all have the capacity to develop an understanding and awareness of the forces—when they affect us or others and take power. In this way we become more adept at managing our lives, supported by the forces and guided from within.

To some degree, an awareness of the life forces is implied in our everyday language. For example, we may refer to the force of an impact, the force of nature, market forces, or a force to be reckoned with. Although each of these phrases does describe a particular force, none of them gives us a true understanding of the nature of the force involved. To discover its nature, we first need to understand each life force and how it affects us. Each level of the life forces hierarchy represents one of our inherent natures: material, vegetative, animal, human, or noble. When something at one of these levels—a genetic predisposition, a feeling, a habit, or a belief—takes power or influences us, whether positively or negatively, it exerts a force.

The model of the life forces will provide you with an interpretive framework for understanding your life. Differentiating between these different forces allows you to discern which elements are influencing you and what needs to be changed or addressed. An awareness of these forces will enable you to see not only the complexity but also the simplicity of life. You will be able to hone your ability to prioritize what is meaningful to you, separate what is important from what is not, and know what supports you as well as what limits or burdens you. When we are supported and served by these forces, we recognize our real needs and how to meet them with a sense of clarity and direction. By surrendering to the One, we can be aligned with and guided by that which is greater than us and transcend our present situation. This is ultimately what slowly assists us in unfolding our human identity.

One afternoon while working on the book, we were beset by an unusually large number of interruptions. The telephone rang incessantly, our computers refused to save information properly, and even the printer mutinied. Finally reaching a point of total frustration, we decided to surrender. Suddenly all became clear: we were experiencing the action of the forces and how we permit them to sidetrack, distract, and frustrate us, rather than allowing the quietness of our inner being to take precedence. Moreover, it was a wonderful reminder to us during the writing of this book that the model of the life forces remains an empirical one until, through our practice of surrender and opening to God, we truly bring it alive throughout our inner being. Only then can our inner understanding and awareness of these forces really grow. We should note that subsequent to our surrender, the phones stopped ringing, our computers worked properly, and the printer produced the requested document!
—Alicia and Alexandra

Being Human

3

The Primary Life Force

There is something like a light within the human self
that can guide people to act in accordance
with the path for their life….

—Muhammad Subuh

*I*n 1986 Alicia and I visited Jerusalem where I had been invited to see a client. The trip appeared a godsend, for it came at a time when I was rather depressed. I had been going through a period where I thought and fantasized about my death. These thoughts had been my close companions for at least a year, and yet I had never articulated these feelings to anyone, let alone Alicia. I had imagined myself dying while performing my prayers in the Al Aqsa mosque in Jerusalem. I had indulged my mind to conjure up all sorts of scenarios over the previous months, but this fantasy capped the lot.

During those months I had been having problems with my prostate, which had become irritated and enlarged, and the memory of my grandfather suffering and then dying from prostate cancer was not very comforting. This was also a time when I was researching and forming the ontological work that I have since taught to many around the world. However, this initial phase was lonely, isolated, and difficult. Many of my old clients left as I practiced this new model of medicine, for they preferred that I simply fix them rather than get them to take responsibility for their illness or state.—Solihin

In Jerusalem, we were staying with the client so that Solihin could treat him on a daily basis. Each day we would go out and explore our surroundings. On our first day we walked through the old city to the Western, or Wailing, Wall, where many Jews were deep in prayer. We walked up the stone steps and through the security checkpoint to the gateway leading to the Temple Mount, which contains the Al Aqsa mosque and the Dome of the Rock. This golden-domed mosque is built on the highest point of the city. Inside, there is an exposed area of rock encircled by a railing in the center of the building. This place is very sacred to Muslims, Jews, and Christians. Jews believe the rock to be the foundation stone of the world, and the pedestal upon which the Ark of the Covenant rested. It is said to be the place where Abraham came to sacrifice his only son, Isaac, before the angel *released him, and where Mohammed had his ascension. It is believed that a footprint in the rock marks that event.*

We had a guide who was explaining the history of the place. He asked if we would like to see the cave below the rock. We knew nothing of this cave, and said yes. He led us around a corner and down some steps into an empty stone cave deep beneath the main floor. As we went down he explained how the cave was believed to have been used as a place of prayer and retreat by many of the prophets, including Abraham, David, Solomon, Elijah and Mohammed.

As we stood there, we became aware of an intense vibration throughout each of us. The guide was ready to leave, and we asked him to meet us outside. We remained in the cave and continued to feel a vibration throughout and around us. This force and experience was not entirely new to us, but receiving this spontaneously was an unexpected gift. It felt very deep and pure, and we understood this to mean that this truly had been a place of surrender to God, and that the force of those prayers and intent was actually contained within this place.

As we talked about this, we realized that this spontaneous experience brought us a sense of Oneness and inner knowing of the Divine, and that it had no language, doctrine or learning associated with it. This pure surrender to God is the content that unites humanity, and the form of religion is often what actually divides it. In a way, the city of Jerusalem symbolizes this as well. There, each of the three major religions has a shared and overlapping history. Each has a belief in the one God, yet each has become deeply divided from the other, making the task of truly coming together seemingly impossible.

It seemed that feeling this deep inner movement that day had opened a part of Solihin to life, and brought alive his faith by allowing him to no longer fear death. The feeling of death that had been pervading his consciousness for so long completely disappeared, and has not returned since.—Alicia

All matter originates and exists only by virtue of a force….We must assume that behind this force is the existence of a conscious and intelligent Mind. This Mind is the matrix of all matter.
—Max Planck

| 17 |

Being Human

Just as the cave contained the palpable essence of the prayers uttered there, within each of us is a *vessel* that contains the essence of who we are. Through life's journey, our vessel is cleaned both within and without by our remembrance of the Divine, our prayers and our surrender. Our thoughts, actions, and feelings then become pure and of love.

The primary life force is also referred to as the Great Life, God, the Source, the Creator, the Divine, Tao, Brahma, Allah, and many other names.

In most philosophical, religious, and spiritual models there exists the concept of that which is beyond all human understanding and all human thought—the Absolute, the Source, the One. From the One emanates a *primary life force* that permeates and connects all of creation. Often our understanding of this force is intellectual rather than experiential and remains a mystery to most of us. Although there are many life forces within and around us, many different religions and philosophies make mention of *the* Life Force. This may refer to the primary life force, which is also called the Great Life, from which all other forces originate. The primary life force exists at all times within all aspects and dimensions of life. Its existence is interpreted differently within the framework of various religions. The primary life force contains both penetrating and enveloping aspects. The penetrating force represents the power of the Creator and has a more masculine and active quality. The enveloping force is Grace, which has a more feminine quality, as it is a force that encloses and envelops life.

Because the penetrating force of the Great Life is most often referred to by mystics who strive for enlightenment, some people assume that only a chosen few will ever experience it; however, many cultures recount stories of spontaneous spiritual experiences—some great, some small—that have occurred across humankind. These stories illustrate that the process of penetration can occur in anyone at any time.

Evidence of the enveloping aspect of the primary life force is present in many different theologies, stories, and myths, as well as in our everyday lives. People often describe intense feelings of the Divine presence of Grace. Many of us have had a moment of complete clarity, a vision, or a dream in which we felt guided. Or, perhaps we sensed a peace and tranquility, the feeling that something sacred was present, a feeling of transcendence, the sudden lifting of a burden, or simply the presence of something beyond ourselves.

I once had a taste of Grace, while staying in a caravanserai—an ancient inn—in the mountains of the Hindu Kush in northern Afghanistan. Leaning against the open window of a second-story mud-brick building, I looked out over the courtyard and sensed how precariously this extremely old resting place was perched on the side of the mountain path. As chickens scratched in the dirt, several donkeys stood placidly, resigned to the midday heat, the animated chatter of the four men squatting on the verandah the only noise in the still air. A young boy crossed the yard, his bare feet raising dust. Suddenly I was filled with a sense of awe. It was as if the whole vista was one; everything contained within it became alive, pulsing and vibrant. We were all inexorably interconnected, the blood in our veins pulsing to a single drum—we were all a part of the whole. It was, I now know, Grace that enveloped all of this and made me part of it, even though I was the stranger.—Solihin

Evidence of Grace is often present in our everyday lives. Shortly after she attended one of our workshops we received the following story from a participant:

I was eating lunch outside with a colleague and telling her about the model of the life forces: the primary life force that penetrates and the force of Grace that envelops. My friend then told a story about Grace. A drunk driver had killed the daughter of an eighty-five-year-old man in an auto accident. The driver, a woman who had a family, was convicted and sent to jail. The victim's father did many things to help the drunk driver's children and was also attempting to get her an early release from jail, because he thought the impact of her being there was negative for her children. After hearing the story I said, "Amazing." And then I said, "I guess that's why they call it Amazing Grace." Just at that moment, the town's church bells rang out "Amazing Grace!"

Amazing grace!
How sweet the sound
That saved a wretch like me!
I once was lost, but now am found,
Was blind, but now I see.
—John Newton

Throughout the ages, seekers of the Truth have sought to expand their consciousness and facilitate their ability to open to the One. Their aspiration has been to taste this Divine force. Most have accomplished this through prayer, reading, and study of the scriptures; others have sought a deepening of their experience through the use of other techniques, exercises, and particular meditations; some have followed the path of surrender or direct experience.

4

The Secondary Life Forces

..within the human self is found,
or exists, a layered arrangement
of forces needed for human life…

—Muhammad Subuh

T he action of the primary life force lies beyond the control of the ordinary human. But acknowledging its place at the top of the life forces hierarchy is essential to understanding that from this force emanate all of the secondary life forces, which support us in our lives. We use the word *secondary* to differentiate between the higher (primary) and the lower (secondary) forces; this does not diminish in any way the importance of the secondary life forces. Each is an integral part of the whole. They are the resources, available to every human, that foster a rich and productive life in which we are able to fulfill our purpose.

The secondary forces have a specific order and distinct function within the hierarchy of the life forces. The idea of a hierarchy often conjures up the notion of increasing value as we move from bottom to top. While the top components typically have more power or responsibility, it is essential that *all* the levels be present and in their proper order for the hierarchy to function effectively.

The secondary life forces exist in all matter, both within the human being and in every element in the world around us. The more complex and sophisticated matter becomes, the wider the range of forces within it. For example, a rock contains only a material force, a plant contains both vegetative and material forces, and a dog contains animal, vegetative, and material forces.

Within human beings are material, vegetative, animal, and human natures. Each of these natures contains a force that brings alive both our outer form and our inner content. That is, each of these forces exist throughout the body, but the influence of each individual force brings alive a different part of our anatomy, physiology, and motor sensory and mental faculties, as well the more subtle aspects of our being. As these forces influence us, they shape and define who we are. They animate us, allow us to move and take action, give us the wherewithal to think, feel, process and integrate our thoughts, and even inspire us.

We can use the metaphor of a house to describe how we operate as human beings in relationship to these forces. Just as we all live in some sort of house in the outer world, our bodies house all the aspects of who we are. The secondary life forces exist within the different levels of the body/house, and each has a particular role and function. These forces act as "servants" who, in an ideal scenario, work together to support us as the owner of the house. In reality, what often happens is that one of these servants operates autonomously. When this occurs, that part has taken charge and is "running the show." By noticing when one or more of these forces have become dominant, we can take steps to return our human house to its rightful order.

Just as the Great Life permeates all of creation, so, too, does it permeate the individual natures within us. This penetrating life force connects, supports, and brings alive each level of the human. If our secondary forces are in balance, the state of our house is then one of harmony and congruency, and we are able to adapt to life's challenges. It is the presence of the Great Life that brings integration and order, widens and expands our lives, illuminates our purpose, and gives us a sense of something greater.

In our outer lives, a congruent state is synonymous with health and wellbeing. The state of our physical, mental, and emotional health at an outer level is a reflection of how we are operating at an inner level. When things go awry within us, they can manifest externally as illness, disease, depression, anxiety, or emotional disorders. These dysfunctions are a key indicator that the servants of the human house are out of order. As we begin to resolve any incongruences that exist within us, we pave the way for resolution to occur at an outer level as well.

*Every object in the world has a spirit and that spirit is **wakan**. Thus the spirits of the tree or things of that kind, while not like the spirit of man, are also wakan.*

—Native American

5

The Five Essential

Qualities

Feet planted firmly in my soil
I widen my consciousness
And gain a new perspective
Ah sweet surrender
That allows me to see
The Light that shines within

*I*n 1987 my colleague and close friend Francois and I were in Austria teaching a kinesiology workshop for teachers who work with children with dyslexia and other learning problems. At the close of the seminar, we decided to demonstrate a rehearsed scenario to our students in order to address a series of "what if?" questions. At one point, I was "supposed" to demonstrate a particular response. Instead, I found myself doing just the op-posite. My failure to follow our predetermined plan was as much a surprise to me as to my partner. It was very embarrassing for Francois, who seemed to have no idea how to proceed. He appeared to be at a loss for words, so I jumped in with some benign explanation of how and why this might occur. We slowly patched up the demonstration and finished the class.

Francois was silent during our long car ride home. Seemingly upset about why I would purposely humiliate him in front of a room full of people, he barely uttered a word. I, too, was feeling bewildered and perplexed as to why I had behaved in such a way. When we arrived at the home of our host, I hurriedly went off to do my prayers. I stood and offered myself to the Creator, to no avail. Nothing seemed to reduce my overwhelming sense of calamity. The sinking feeling in my stomach made me face the fact that I needed to talk this through with Francois.

We spoke openly; I of the mystery of why I had behaved as such, and he of his sense of betrayal of trust. In our attempt to understand what had happened, we began to argue, each of us steadfastly maintaining our own position. In the heat of accusation and counteraccusation, we saw that we needed help and decided to stand back and surrender to God, asking for guidance. In the ensuing quiet, we asked for some understanding of why this had happened. Through repeated surrender and subsequent reflection we were given a very real and dramatic understanding of our particular situation.

In my surrender I experienced the elements of flexibility and reflectiveness, and my own state regarding these two qualities. At a metaphorical level it was as if my flexibility had taken on a protective quality, like a snake coiled *around my heart, making it dangerous for people to become emotionally close to me. This related to our situation in the workshop, where Francois and I had become close, and this protective part of me had struck out in order to maintain a distance; hence I sabotaged our demonstration. My agility of thought and quickness of mind gave the impression of width and openness, but actually they were only ploys to keep people satisfied and to obfuscate the truth of what had really happened. In a similar vein, I saw that my reflective capacity was rather contained and narrow, almost as if I were held to the ground, vulture-like, picking at things that were dead or moribund, unable to truly rise up and see the bigger picture. I felt that my ability to see was often impaired by my wounded state, like that of a eagle with a broken wing, which I interpreted as some aspect of my reflective mind being unable to "take flight."*

Later that night, as we walked in the Vienna woods and talked about our experience together, we became very excited by what we had been shown. We realized that we were making sense of fifteen or more years of inner growth and spiritual experience. Our "soil" had been prepared to receive this new seed of understanding, and this experience opened up a whole new paradigm.

As we talked and reflected upon what had happened, I suddenly realized that I had experienced two of the elements of the caduceus. The caduceus is a symbol that is used in various forms in the different branches of medicine. It consists of three elements, which are described classically as a staff or wand, around which are entwined either one or two snakes, and a pair of wings. To most people it is simply an icon that implicitly represents the medical profession. My own training and journey through osteopathic medicine had given me a familiarity with the caduceus and its elements, and through this vision and experience I was now ready to understand this icon from a completely different perspective. I now saw the staff as representing integrity, the snakes as flexibility and the wings as reflectiveness. This was a revelation, for what I had witnessed firsthand was the action of the life forces; I had tasted a living symbol, as opposed to a material or static icon. I had experienced the caduceus within me, which had shown me something about my own state.

I understood the message clearly; I was stuck, unable to rise up from my family pattern of protecting a wounded heart. Consequently, I used my flexibility (the snake) to become adept in my thinking, actions, and words, covertly keeping people from coming too close. This limited my ability to be truly reflective so that I could see why I acted as I did. Subsequently, I became aware that I hadn't been shown anything that day about my integrity. I realized that this was a part of me that was largely unformed, still dormant, which prevented me from being able to pinpoint why I acted in particular ways. My lack of clarity stopped me from disentangling myself from this family pattern of keeping love away. I was so entangled in this dynamic that I was unable to see what was going on, to rise above it, or cut through it. As we teach in all our workshops, without integrity (the staff), our flexibility (the snake) has nothing to climb up, nor does our reflectiveness (the eagle) have something to come down to perch or roost upon.

This experience gave Francois and me the opportunity to reflect upon and begin to integrate all the information that we had received. As a result, we were able to recognize for the first time the relationship between the caduceus and the life forces, and began to see a way to present this understanding to others.—Solihin

The symbol of the caduceus has an interesting history that dates back thousands of years. Although there is much scholarly debate regarding the meaning of this symbol, the generally accepted interpretation is that the staff or wand represents integration, alignment, wholeness, and a connection between heaven and earth; the snake signifies animation, transformation, duality, and movement; and the wings symbolize thought, imagination, and spirituality. Today, the caduceus is widely recognized as an icon of medicine and healing. Even if you have not considered its deeper meaning, you are probably aware of its presence on ambulances, hospitals, and other medical establishments.

The image of the snakes and a staff appears in myths and stories from many different cultures. Aesculapius, the son of Apollo, recognized as the Greek god of medicine and healing, carried a rough-hewn staff entwined by a single snake. Hermes, the messenger of the gods in Greek mythology, known for both his cunning and eloquence in speech, was said to have thrown his magic wand at two fighting snakes that became entwined around it and then ceased to fight.

In Roman mythology, it was Mercury who used a magic snake-entwined wand given to him by Apollo.

The elements of a staff, snake, and wings combine to form a dynamic representation of human qualities. This symbol is archetypal, both individually and collectively, and it summons from the unconscious associations that are filtered through our personal histories, familial patterns and cultural heritages.

The fact that one mythological character carries a staff entwined with two snakes and the other a staff with just a single snake tells us something about life. The dual snakes remind us that in all of life there exists a duality such as light/dark, separation/unity, on/off, full/empty, high/low, active/passive, right/wrong, inner/outer, and masculine/feminine. Duality, like the life forces, exists everywhere. A portion of the earth is in darkness while its other half basks in light; a high tide comes into shore, a low tide goes out to sea. We, too, have a duality within our own bodies in the double helix of our DNA, and in our left and right brain hemispheres which have complimentary but differing ways of processing information. This duality is evident even in the division of the One, the Absolute, into the penetrating and enveloping forces.

Although these examples of duality are very clear, we contain within us dualities in feelings, actions and thoughts that are much more subtle and harder to discern. In everyday life we are constantly confronted with choices that cause our feelings, actions, and responses to vacillate, or swing back and forth. When we metaphorically tip the scales to one extreme or the other, we become out of balance.

In reality, the unity of our dual natures results from the presence of true integrity. Just as a pendulum moves rhythmically from side to side, yet always returns to the stillness of the central point, integrity provides the central axis that unifies our nature. In this stillness the two snakes representing our dual nature become one. The single snake-entwined staff of Aesculapius symbolizes this aligning and unifying quality.

In the Chinese yin/yang symbol, yin represents the un-illuminated side of a hill, and yang denotes the side bathed in sunlight.

| 29 |

Solihin's experience in Vienna was pivotal to our recognition that the caduceus represents the qualities that need to be embodied internally for the development of a dynamic human being. In our work over the last fifteen years, we have expanded on the original components of integrity, flexibility, and reflectiveness and added the two additional elements of surrender and value, which are symbolized by a dove and a gem. These represent innate qualities and aspects of our nature. Moreover, at an inner level they illustrate aspects of the Divine that bring our humanity alive. Some of these qualities may be quite apparent within us, while others might still be dormant or hidden. Each quality enables us to navigate the human journey and expand our personal map. These are *the five essential qualities.*

A staff, which symbolizes integrity
A single snake around the staff, which symbolizes flexibility
A pair of wings, which symbolize reflectiveness
A dove, which symbolizes surrender
A gem, which symbolizes value

Each of these five essential qualities is multifaceted and operates at both an inner and outer level, supporting us by fostering our relationship with all the different parts of ourself: our body, feelings, actions, thoughts, and essence. Each quality acts as a bridge by facilitating movement from level to level within the life forces hierarchy. It is integrity that allows us to be firmly connected to and aligned with our body, feelings, actions, thoughts, ancestry, and, at an inner level, with God. Flexibility provides a resilient body, an adaptive physiology, the ability to transform, and a width of thought and experience; it brings our inner feelings alive. Reflectiveness enables us to step back and see the big picture, to see ourselves, discern our feelings, observe our actions, view our choices, and be illuminated at an inner level. Through surrender we can open to the Divine and find trust, faith, patience, sincerity, union and—eventually—a sense of our own value.

Surrender is perhaps the most important tool humans possess in our endeavor to find the nobility in ourselves. You will see references to surrender throughout this book. By far its most important aspect is the willingness to stand and do our best to offer ourselves to God, even if we do not feel particularly adept. Most of us have experienced times when we feel discouraged, have doubts and struggles, or feel that surrender is actually the last thing we want to do. When we are able to find that quietness and place of surrender, we can overcome the different obstacles that get in the way, and reaffirm our connection to the Creator.

When we surrender, we become both open and receptive to the possibility of receiving a response. It could be a thought, vision, movement, or bodily sensation that helps to pinpoint, animate, or illuminate something. Our human cognition will take what we have just experienced and apply some sort of understanding to what we have been shown.

It is through surrender that we pave the way for the development of the five essential qualities, including surrender itself. In our surrender we make space for the inner development of these qualities. In stillness we employ an open mind, cease habitual actions, relinquish restrictive emotions and feelings, and separate from old or cultural dictates. Tuning in to the wavelength of the Great Life allows us to become connected, alive, and animated, and to receive a knowing beyond our education or experiences. This wisdom is given to us, rather than fabricated through our thoughts. It is then that we begin to see the true value of all things, and we may receive in some way, small or large, a sense of our own inner value.

We depict the life forces and the five essential qualities as a hierarchy to simplify an otherwise complex idea. In its truest sense, however, the model of the life forces is multidimensional and mirrors the intricacies and complexities of the human being, the cosmos, and life itself. The life forces can also be represented as a series of concentric spheres which are drawn as circles. Beginning with the material, each subsequent circle—vegetative, animal, human, and noble—is larger than the one preceding it, as its potential influence is greater. The five essential qualities, which bridge the different levels, act as spokes that penetrate through and organize all the circles. This illustrates how the different aspects of the Divine enter, bring alive, illuminate, and widen us, giving us a taste of our value. We can taste these Divine attributes in any order as we cultivate, develop, and practice these human qualities. This is why different people have different experiences: they experience the Divine in different ways and at different times. One person's journey is not necessarily linear or similar to another's.

Modern quantum physics looks upon all systems—whether submolecular, cellular, global, a solar system or the entire universe—as self-organizing and living. These organizing forces are implicit in the five essential qualities. They constantly "reorganize" us as humans.

| 31 |

6

The Material Self

Within every human is contained a sacred promise:
the commitment to connect with the Creator
and carry out the Divine instructions for our life.
This original challenge is the impetus
to arise from our "clay," the material aspect of who we are,
and allow God to shape us according to the Divine plan.

T he material level is the foundation of the life forces hierarchy. It encompasses a broad range of elements, all of which relate to matter, whether manmade or naturally occurring. For most of us the word "material" probably brings to mind things in our external environment such as money, houses, cars, clothing, jewelry, and other possessions. Like all matter, these things have a force, which may or may not affect us. When the material force predominates, as is often evident in western cultures, this fuels a continual need and desire to acquire more and more. We then derive our sense of value from material possessions and wealth.

He who knows he has enough is rich.

—Lao-tzu

While external objects are an important aspect of the material level, they are only one part of the story. We are often so preoccupied with them that we overlook another essential element: our own internal material resources, the most valuable of which come from our lineage. Apart from the heirlooms that have been passed down over generations, many of us are unaware of the inherent resources that we have been given by our ancestors: their cultural and spiritual heritages, achievements, struggles, strengths, weaknesses, joys, and sorrows all shape and color who we are. The fabric of our being is a rich tapestry woven from the threads of the life experiences of those who have gone before. Using the qualities bestowed upon us by our ancestors enables us to arise from our material nature while still maintaining our connection to it.

My feelings are that in each family there is one who seems called to find the ancestors. To put flesh on their bones and make them live again, to tell the family story and to feel that somehow they know and approve.

—Della M. Cummings-Wright

Our physical bodies are composed of material elements in the form of tissue, bone, muscle, and organs. These are shaped via the blueprint of our DNA, which is supplied by our parents and illustrates the essential nature of that genetic coding. Although the force of our coding is most evident in our physical features and shapes, it also influences our character, traits, and predispositions to illness or good health.

In recent years, scientific research on identical twins has verified that DNA influences our psychological, mental, and emotional aspects. Studies describe identical twins separated since birth that were reunited in adulthood after being raised in very different environments. In addition to their corresponding physical characteristics, researchers discovered many astounding similarities in their psyches, tastes, habits, and emotions. In contrast to previous theories, these studies have demonstrated that the force of our genetic coding plays a more substantial role in our development than the force of our external environment.

Every cell of your body carries your familial predispositions. Your structure may hold you in a posture that is similar to that of your father, or you may have your mother's sluggish digestive system. You may take on an indolent approach to life, as have those of past generations on one side of your family, and yet the brilliance of your thinking may resemble another family member. You may inherit your mother's honesty, your father's tenacity, and perhaps your grandfather's thriftiness, or lack thereof!

> We had just finished a workshop in Vienna and had gone away for a few days to celebrate our anniversary. We were at a traditional spa on the Austro-Hungarian border. One morning, while we were recovering on our loungers, pink and gently steaming after a sauna, four generations of the same family passed by. As is typical in European spas everyone was completely naked, giving us an opportunity to notice what might not have otherwise been so clear! All four generations of this family–from the elders down to the children–had a similar and very particular shape and stoop. It was a great illustration of the strength of genetic coding.–Alicia

The material world is composed of billions of vibrating atoms, each bound together in their orbit by minuscule electromagnetic forces. Every atom oscillates at a specific frequency, and the sum of all of this atomic vibration is known as a *resonance*. Every human being resonates at a unique constitutional frequency according to what is carried in his or her DNA. A story about our colleague, Tomas, demonstrates the strength of this genetic resonance. Adopted as a baby, Tomas displayed an early talent for music; spontaneously playing the piano at age three, he outgrew his teacher by the time he was eight. He also demonstrated a keen interest in the design and function of buildings. When he met his birth mother as an adult, he discovered that she was a musician and that his birth father was an architect. He found that he was very similar to his mother in looks, temperament, and humor. When he later met his father, he also recognized many common traits. Although he was happy growing up in his adoptive family, he had

Too many people spend money they haven't earned, to buy things they don't want, to impress people they don't like.

—Will Rogers

| 35 |

always somehow felt "different." Meeting his birth parents gave him a sense of his place in the world and a connection to his familial "soil."

Human beings have an unconscious awareness of the resonance of others. This is what some people refer to as "vibes". When we are attracted to someone whose force is similar to our own, it is because we resonate at a similar frequency.

What we carry within our genetic coding is the base material of our potential. For this reason, we refer to the material level of the life forces hierarchy as the "basement" of the human house. In most homes, the basement is where, over time, we store things and accumulate "stuff." The same is true of our genetic basements, which contain the DNA, or "soil," that forms the foundation from which we arise. Its force permeates our entire being, shaping and defining who we are as unique individuals. Stored within our basements are the ideas, maps, beliefs, feelings, behavioral patterns, spiritual or religious traditions, ethnic roots, and cultural customs that we have inherited and with which we resonate. While some of these are obvious to us, others remain dormant or hidden. Various events in our lives may, over time, act as triggers that activate these genetic tendencies and initiate changes that subtly alter our feelings, actions, and thoughts.

Our familial soil contains many seeds that may lie dormant until events in our life water them into development.

Most basements are not well lit, and we often view them as places that are dark, creepy, cluttered, and disorganized. Sooner or later, something usually happens to prompt us to clean out the basement. When we finally muster the fortitude to clean it, we can take stock of its contents and see what is and is not needed. It is then transformed from a place that is in disarray to one that is orderly and free from clutter, and it becomes a valuable resource, the contents of which we can access at will. Often feeling the need to clean this clutter parallels a desire to clean something inside ourselves. By making the intention to clean the basement of our homes we can reflect or initiate the intention to clean our inner "basements." Whenever we clear out old stuff, we make space for something new.

Many participants in our workshops have described with great joy the results of the process of cleaning out their basements after years of neglect. They described feeling lighter, less burdened, and liberated from that which was no longer needed. One woman rented an industrial-sized dumpster and spent her vacation filling it to the brim. She told us that although it was extremely hard work, she felt completely energized after finishing the task. You might want to try cleaning your own home's basement to see how it makes you feel.

If you happen to live in an apartment or home without a basement, any storage area will do!

At a practical level, it is far easier to clean the basement of a house than to clean our internal basement; but many of the steps involved are the same. The first step in cleaning our human basement is to notice what it contains. We often don't recognize our inner resources simply because we have not yet taken stock of them. One way to do this is to know your family story and the personal histories of your forebears. Even if you do not have access to this information, it is of paramount importance to know your own ontology—your personal story and the events and experiences that have brought you to the place where you now are in your life. This will enable you to recognize both the beneficial qualities that you possess and those that are limiting.

A client came to see Solihin on one of his visits to the east coast. She was depressed, lacked energy, and felt very stuck in her life. As he worked with her, it became clear that she needed to address old inherited patterns. Solihin asked her if she had a basement. "Yes," she said, "Not one, but two, and they are completely full!" It was evident that the force of what she carried—old ideas, familial patterns and old feelings that prevented her from being able to move forward in her life. She left with a homework assignment—to go home and clean out both her basements. Some months later she returned to see him again. Solihin was surprised to see that there was no change in her situation— until she admitted that she had not cleaned out her basements. A few months later she returned for a third time. Things had really changed in her life. She had lost weight, enrolled in massage school, and had a new relationship. She had cleaned out both her basements, and subsequently other things in her life had started to shift. Her inner life mirrored what she had been able to do in her outer life, so that the old patterns in her coding were no longer dominant.

Sometimes, the force of our coding can render us immobile, creating a heaviness or burden that we describe as feeling stuck or unable to move forward in our lives.

Several years ago, I went through a period of time where I was feeling rather stuck. I felt as though I needed something to change, but wasn't sure what. We were visiting New York City, and had spent the day with my three brothers–a very unusual occurrence, as only one lives in New York, one lives in Australia, and the other lives in England. That evening, in celebration of our daughter Miriam's birthday, we enjoyed a delicious meal at a famous Belgian restaurant that specialized in mussels. The next morning Solihin and I awoke feeling slightly sick. We were teaching a one-day workshop in the city, so went ahead as planned. As the day progressed, he felt better and I felt worse. That evening we retreated to our son's apartment to watch a movie while everyone else went out. I started to feel very ill, hot, weak, and nauseous. When we got up to leave at the end of the evening, I could hardly stand and felt terrible. By the time we got downstairs, I felt incapable of walking to the taxi waiting by the curb.

Somehow I managed to get to the car. The next thing I was aware of was the taxi driver asking if we needed to go to the hospital, as I had apparently just had a seizure! I felt quite scared, as nothing like this had ever happened to me before. As I felt myself drifting off again, I kept saying, "Help me God," and holding onto Solihin in an effort to ground myself. To make matters even worse, a few minutes later our taxi crashed into another car. We weren't hurt, but had to change to another taxi to get home.

The next day I was unable to eat and felt very fragile. A couple of times I felt as if I might drift off again. By now it was clear that my seizure was a result of severe food poisoning from the mussels, as the bacteria that make us sick produce neurotoxins within the body after twenty-four hours. Although several of us had eaten from the same plate, we all reacted differently. Our son Lachlan and daughter Rebecca both became violently ill during the day but managed to effectively void their systems. Solihin spent the day simply looking rather "green." This demonstrates how we all have differing capacities to handle something that could be a threat to our health. Lachlan and Rebecca were both able to get rid of it; Solihin managed to transform it into something that had no major impact; I held onto it until it became a serious threat.

As I began to recover, I reflected upon what this experience was showing me. It was interesting that I had spent the day prior to the seizure with

all my brothers, the masculine element of my original family. I had been very aware of my father during the entire weekend. He was a wonderful man who had passed away many years before. He sometimes had difficulty recognizing and utilizing his own resources. I realized that I, too, carried that same family pattern in relation to being able to transform—in this case, to transform a potent bacteria into something more benign.

As a result of this experience, something shifted inside me. I was able to take action to lose weight, which was something that had been an obstacle, both for my father and me. Since that time I have initiated new projects and done several things that I have never done before.—Alicia

Your genetic coding provides you with a basic operating system in which your neurology has been hardwired to process information in a particular way. This operating system has been shaped and modified by every generation of your ancestors. When it does not know how to process something, it becomes overloaded and shuts down (switches off).

When faced with a life-threatening situation, the reptilian hindbrain, the most primitive part of the human brain, switches off all activity except that which keeps us alive. It sends the subconscious message "do not move, breathe, or blink, or you will be seen and attacked!" Our response is to become silent, barely moving, almost invisible. You will notice this in a reptile house at the zoo; it is often difficult to see a crocodile, alligator, or lizard, or to believe that they are alive, as their movements are barely perceptible.

We can also switch off in far less dire circumstances when something overloads or threatens our system, whether internally or externally. Often we unconsciously switch off when something does not feel good, or when we fear what is about to be revealed, refuse to face an uncomfortable issue, or simply lose interest in what is going on. When this happens, we may notice that we have lost our train of thought or suddenly realize that we are not present any more. We may become sleepy, or suddenly yawn, speak in a monotone voice, or feel flat, bored, stuck, separate, or unable to see things in any way other than black or white. We become inanimate, closed to change or possibility.

Our switching mechanism parallels the main fuse box for the electrical system of a house: when it gets overloaded, it blows a fuse and switches off. The same applies to our human houses. When you notice that you have switched off, you are metaphorically in the basement, which means that you have defaulted to your basic operating system, or the dictates of your genetic coding. The paradox is that although we can easily switch off, we do not so easily switch on again. The first step is to notice where you are—in the darkness of the basement—then switch on the lights to see what has brought you there, and what you need to do to get out.

Just as a pearl is formed as a result of an irritation within the oyster, sometimes things that are in the shadows will irritate us until we see their value, or the resource that we contain.

When our material force supports and serves us, it acts as a record keeper. We sometimes refer to ourselves as being "in the dark" in regard to a particular circumstance. The role and function of the record keeper is to ensure that the basement lights are switched on and that we have access to the resources stored there, such as our genetic instructions, inherited memories, and experiences from our own life. When the record keeper serves us, we have the capacity to access, route, and process data stored in our cellular matrix.

Even when our basement is illuminated, however, some things remain in the shadows. These shadows conceal old memories or the inherited parts of us that, for some reason, we do not want to see or recognize. We often regard them as the things that we would rather not remember, or our shortcomings, deficiencies, or weaknesses. Nevertheless, attempting to avoid them does not negate the forces associated with them. They subtly continue to affect our state, particularly at a subconscious level. When they take power, we might notice that we repeatedly do things that do not support us, or that take us down the same unproductive path. This is when we are "gripped" by the material force that sabotages our ability to rise up out of the old and come alive by moving into the new. When we face and illuminate our shadows they lose their force and instead become a resource that can support us by showing us something about ourselves.

Sometimes we would rather shut the basement door and walk away than face things that we perceive as negative. For example, there is often the desire to distance ourselves from our parents and our roots. Even if we physically remove ourselves from these influences, which can diminish their force, we still contain their resonance within our DNA, so we never actually escape them! Markus, a participant in our Austrian workshops, tried to avoid the limitations of a family pattern by going to the opposite extreme. He soon discovered that this was equally limiting:

> *My family immigrated from Romania to Germany, which they saw as a paradise. When they arrived they had nothing, and it took three generations of working very hard to become successful. Everyone in my family now has large houses, lots of money, and works all the time. At the age of seventy-six my father earned an M.A. in business and still works every day. I did the opposite, because I didn't want to be like him. I didn't work, didn't study, did nothing. Only now am I able to see the resource of being able to work hard, but not to the exclusion of everything else. I can see the importance of utilizing my resources rather than being a slave to them.*

Sometimes we dwell on what we perceive as the less positive aspects of our ancestry, rather than seeing the value of what we have been given. By focusing on the negative we narrow our perspective. If we are able to step back and become reflective, however, we can then consider what lies beyond an event or behavior—the ontology, or sequence of events, that led to it. By seeing what forces were at play, we might recognize that we, too, carry this same dynamic. We can then make changes to alter that pattern and stop the cycle of passing it on to our own descendants. Often our irritation with others or with a situation parallels something similar in ourselves. This human action of being willing to own, rather than blame, allows us to begin the process of forgiveness, which is the genesis of healing.

Noticing and acknowledging that some aspects within us tend to be limiting is the first step to moving beyond them.

Ala'din

The allegorical story of Ala'din illustrates many elements of the material level. This tale is part of *The Thousand and One Nights*, a compilation of teaching stories that have circulated in the Middle East for hundreds of years. Below we have retold part of the tale; in its entirety, Ala'din's story details many more of his adventures.

In a city called Baghdad in a faraway land lived a young ne'er-do-well named Ala'din. His father had failed in his attempts to encourage his son to accompany him in his business. Due to economic circumstances Ala'din's father found life difficult, and because he was not supported by his son, he gave up and died. He left his wife, a seamstress, with nothing save her indolent and rather lost son and her own skills, to provide the little money that the two lived upon.

A magician from Africa came across Ala'din as he mingled in the bazaar, and he pretended to be the long lost brother of the boy's father. He gave Ala'din and his mother money, new clothes, and food, and managed to seduce them both into believing his story. One day he took Ala'din up into the mountains, and upon making a fire, uttered some incantations. Suddenly a large stone emerged from the desert floor to reveal a dark opening, and within it a cave. The terrified Ala'din tried to escape, but the clever magician hit him hard, stupefying him, and then persuaded him to go down into the cave to retrieve an old lamp. The magician told him to go deep into the farthest corner of the cave where he would find forty-nine steps. These steps, he said, would lead to a door and a room, within which he would find the lamp. Giving Ala'din his ring as a talisman, he warned him not to take anything else from the cave, even if it appeared to be of value.

The distressed boy went into the cave, and although he noticed the sparkling jewels and gold and silver treasures that littered the ground, he did not take any.

Finding the stairs, he descended and found the door, which he opened. Inside the room he found a rather dirty lamp, which he picked up and placed under his clothing. He headed back through the cave, but the luster and sparkle of the gems were so enticing that, despite the magician's warning, he filled his pockets with them along the way. Eventually he returned to the entrance. The magician, looming tall above him, demanded that he give him the lamp, but Ala'din asked to first be helped out of the cave. The magician couldn't lift him out for he was so heavy, weighed down by what he had collected. He again demanded the lamp. Ala'din steadfastly refused to give it up, and the two struggled. Ala'din hung precariously, holding the magician's arm by one hand. Suddenly, strangers appeared in the valley, and the magician, fearing discovery, let go, and once again intoned a command to close the cave, imprisoning Ala'din.

Left inside the dark, musty, impenetrable cave, Ala'din slumped dejectedly into a heap and wondered about his fate. He absentmindedly fiddled with the ring that he had been given. Suddenly there was a rush of smoke and fire, and a genie appeared. The genie told the terrified boy that he was at his command and would obey Ala'din's every word. Ala'din, seeing his chance to escape, asked the genie to transport him out of the cave. In a flash he was back home with his equally startled mother, who looked askance at the sudden appearance of her son.

He soothed his mother by producing the lamp from his pocket. As he rubbed it to polish off the dust and grime, he was amazed at the appearance of another genie. Bowing low to him, the genie told Ala'din that he was now his owner. The boy, seeing the opportunity before him, asked the genie of the lamp to produce food for his mother. In the twinkling of an eye, a sumptuous feast appeared on golden plates. The following day Ala'din went into the bazaar to sell some of the gold plates. Although the jeweler who bought them cheated him, Ala'din was jubilant to receive this sudden effortless windfall.

Over the ensuing months, the two lived off the jewels that he had taken from the cave. Gradually, Ala'din learned to sell the remaining pieces for a fair price, as his father's talent for business began to emerge in him. He eventually became successful and well liked in his community.

Ala'din's journey into the cave symbolizes the process of discovering our own internal resources. Although he found what he thought were precious jewels, they actually weighed him down and burdened him so that he was unable to leave the cave. Both genies (*jinn* in Arabic) appeared out of smoke and fire, two elements that symbolize transformation. They represent resources, often overlooked, that we contain in our genetic coding. Utilizing them not only enabled Ala'din to escape his predicament (the sealed cave), but also to access the resource (business acumen) that enabled him to provide for himself and his mother in a way that he had previously been unable to do.

Within every human is a vessel that is the container of the essence of our Self. This vessel is represented by Ala'din's lamp. For many of us, the connection to this part of ourselves and knowledge of its real value, or even of its existence, may have been lost. Ala'din's journey into the cave symbolizes our own journey into the cave of our material nature. Just as Ala'din had to find a new resource to help him escape from of the cave, we too have to find the part of us that can help us move beyond our limitations. When we cling to cherished ideas, habits, or traits, they can become the jewels that weigh us down and prevent us from moving forward. What is needed may be something unexpected, something that has thus far remained hidden from us. When we endeavor to know the contents of our cave, we will eventually find the vessel that we have each inherited from our lineage. It has always been there, but it may have been discarded or simply put away, forgotten.

As with Ala'din, the value of the vessel may not initially be obvious to us until we polish and clean it and can see what lies beneath its layers of tarnish. The metaphor of polishing the vessel reminds us that worship of the Divine brings us alive. In fact, the root meaning of the Arabic word *Ala'din*, is "excellence in religion." When we surrender and allow the Divine to enter and clean our vessel, our own innate resources, as well as our shadows, are illuminated. This human quest to truly become ourselves is not easy. It might at times seem impossible to move beyond the familiar, yet somewhat restrictive environment of our own cave. Like a butterfly emerging from the chrysalis, we must accept that it takes time and effort to transform.

7

Integrity

Grounded in the legacy of my ancestors I stand
In union with the Source, with life itself
As stillness and quiet arise within
I hear the Call that guides me on life's journey.

The presence of integrity is essential for all the other levels of the life forces hierarchy to be aligned and integrated. It acts as a bridge between the material and vegetative levels, bringing unity, wholeness, and uprightness to a human being. The staff of integrity symbolizes the central axis that supports all the other elements of the caduceus. When firmly connected to our familial soil, integrity allows us to arise from our material nature into our feeling self. This brings the memories, ideas, and resources from our roots up into our awareness, so that we have a firm idea of who we are and what we stand for.

When you are upright, your integrity gives you the connection to your internal self, your ancestral resources, and God. In practical terms, as we accept and acknowledge our familial history, patterns, and spiritual foundation we start to own who we are. The idea of connecting to our familial history, our roots, is an important one; ironically, only by connecting to our foundation can we find the resources needed to rise above the force of our genetic predispositions and tendencies. Moreover, without this connection, we are much more susceptible to the influence of external forces. Our integrity will then waiver, and we will become unstable; like a post that is not set firmly in the ground, or a tree that has shallow roots, we can be easily tilted or knocked over.

When integrity emerges from within, it carries dignity, power, and clarity, much like the pronouncements of the prophet Solomon, when he rendered judgment on two mothers fighting over a child. Upon the death of her child, one of the mothers had stolen the other's child and claimed it was her own. Solomon ordered his soldiers to cut the child in half. One of the women agreed to this, but the other immediately became distraught and begged Solomon to give the child to the other woman rather than have it killed. Solomon, recognizing that a real mother would preserve the life of her child at all costs, awarded the child to that woman.

True integrity is the inner connection that begins the process of finding our path back to the Source. Obviously, it is difficult, if not impossible, to measure or gauge one's own inner integrity. We can practice the outer *form* of integrity in our daily lives, however, by standing firm, speaking our truth, respecting our self and others, and integrating our thoughts, words, and actions with clarity and purpose. As we do this, we are preparing the soil for the germination and growth of our inner integrity—our *content*. In reality, this means we are constantly present, aware, attentive, and mindful of living a sacred life, which aligns us with the Great Life. This again highlights the essential relationship between our inner and outer selves.

In our everyday world, outer symbols of integrity are seen in such things as a conductor's baton, the scepter of a king or queen, and the crosier of a bishop. For most of us, our first introduction to integrity was when we began to learn right from wrong. Perhaps this was by the raised finger of a parent or teacher who scolded us, or, conversely, by experiencing a feeling of having done the right thing. A few of us may have defied authority and witnessed firsthand the integrity that was symbolized by a judge's gavel. As parents, some of us may have tried to exemplify integrity through stern methods of discipline. On a more global level, government leaders sometimes attempt to demonstrate their integrity by "wielding a big stick" to beat down an opponent. It is important to note that simply displaying some external form of integrity does not necessarily reflect its presence at an inner level.

Engage in Torah and charity. Even with an ulterior motive, the habit of right doing will lead also to right motivation.
—Judaism Talmud, Pesahim 50b

At a physical level, our spine and posture reflect the state of our integrity. Even our language mirrors this, as we often refer to those who take authority and stand up for themselves as having "backbone" and those who lack substance and fortitude as "spineless." Spinal problems and inherited traits such as scoliosis, a bowed back, or susceptibility to backache may indicate the need to address issues related to integrity.

Integrity is the connection that gives us a sense of trust in the Creator.

One of our colleagues, Beata, was born with a spinal deformity, and thus a tendency for scoliosis, or curvature of the spine. When she was fourteen years old, she had surgery to fuse seven vertebrae in the mid to upper part of her back. Her spine was fused at a forty-five degree angle.

It was not until I began to study the life forces that I saw the connection between integrity and the spine. I began to understand that I needed to pay attention to what would prompt my spine to curve and twist. As I became more and more aware of this, the extraordinary began. My fused spine (I do not have any metal rods) began to straighten. Now, most people would not even know that I have a scoliosis.

My understanding of the life forces has helped me to begin to recognize what I turn away from or turn towards, versus facing forward. My spine has become more flexible and basically pain-free unless I put myself under some new stress. Now if my spine becomes stiff or I sense myself "turning," I pause for a moment and do my best to listen inside as to why. I have thus become more connected to myself in the process. Not only has my spine straightened, but with that physical integrity, I found that it was easier for me to have a voice and speak my truth, to know what I am feeling, to face and engage with people on all levels.—Solihin

There are said to be two kinds of people in the world, those who find connections between things and those who draw a line to separate. The same line that connects can also be the line that separates.

Neurological dysfunction also signifies a loss of connection and therefore a compromised integrity of the nervous system. Neurological illnesses may illustrate this loss of neural competency. The body illustrates a loss of connection at some level by disorganizing the nervous system. Similarly, in a less striking way, losing a train of thought, failing to make eye contact with another, or feeling unable to be still and present may also indicate a loss of integrity or connection.

Many of us will recall the story *The Emperor's New Clothes*, in which an emperor desired a new and very special outfit for an important parade. The tailors who came to measure him promised to make the most exquisite and richly decorated costume in the kingdom. They emphasized the unique quality of these clothes—they would be visible only to those of elevated status and rank. Anyone who was unable to see them would be proved unfit for office or unpardonably stupid. When the time came for the emperor to be fitted, there was nothing to be seen. The emperor did not want to appear unfit for office or unpardonably stupid, however, so he responded with approval as the tailor "displayed" the fabric and the work in progress. All his courtiers joined him in admiring the new clothes, as they, too, did not want to appear stupid. Finally, the parade day came and the streets were lined with people waiting to see the emperor's special clothes. As the parade passed, everyone was oohing and aahing over them, until a young boy said in a very loud and clear voice "but the emperor isn't wearing any clothes!" Whereupon everyone gasped, as they suddenly saw the truth—that the emperor was clad only in his underwear!

We often find it far easier to go with the flow than to stand up for our beliefs when they differ from others', especially those of people in a position of authority. *The Emperor's New Clothes* shows how easily we follow the herd or go along with the collective by allowing our integrity to be usurped by the force of someone else's "authority." Sometimes in innocence there is a clarity that cuts through the pomp, circumstance, and superficial "fluff" that obscures the truth. This is integrity.

None of us is immune from moments when our actions reflect the loss of integrity. For example, if we do not correct someone who has undercharged us, if we don't keep our word, or if we lie for personal gain, we have allowed external forces to sway our integrity. Our susceptibility to the force of others' words or beliefs can also take us off center.

Through integrity we can begin to pinpoint the origins of why we feel the way we do, why we act in particular ways, and why our thoughts pursue certain pathways or tracks.

> When I was younger, I found it quite hard to stand up for myself or to confront someone else. I definitely lacked a sense of connection to myself. There were times when I felt that I didn't even know what I thought of a situation or belief and would see what other people said before making up my mind. As I grew older, the need to express my true feelings also grew. The difficulty was that often when I did, the sometimes negative reaction I got would affect my feelings and make me doubt their value, preventing me from taking what I felt was appropriate action.

> During a workshop many years ago, a woman said something in the group and then later contradicted herself. Although no one else seemed to notice, as cofacilitator, I felt the need to ask her about it. In front of the group, she denied that she had made any conflicting statements. Although I knew she wasn't telling the truth, a part of me started to question whether I had made a mistake. After all, no one else had noticed. During a break, the woman approached me and admitted that she had lied and tried to cover it up. I was able to see how my feelings of being uncomfortable, or possibly wrong, and how my lack of connection to myself, my truth, had made me waiver when I was confronted with a difficult situation.

Integrity is like a sword that allows us to cleanly and decisively cut away that which is not needed.

Over the years, my connection to myself has gradually developed and my sense of clarity has grown. I am now able to be clear with others without doubting myself, and am less swayed by the force of someone else when challenged.—Alicia

Some of us may develop one particular aspect of our integrity, such as having a sharp and precise mind, a highly tuned, healthy and muscular body, or feelings that are intuitive or highly receptive. By doing this, however, we may neglect the other parts of ourselves. Even our relationship to the Divine may reflect this. Rather than making it an integrated part of our lives, we might feel that in order to be "spiritual" we must bypass the other parts of ourselves. By not paying attention to them, we overlook how essential they are to the wholeness of our being. It is integrity that unifies and integrates all these different parts of ourselves, and which provides the pathway towards the inner feeling of life. This places order in the hierarchy as all the elements align in their proper positions.

Integrity brings into line the past, the present, and the future.

The essential quality of integrity is the prerequisite for the development of our capacity to taste and feel the Great Life. Contained deep within all humans is the longing to return to the Source. This hunger within prompts us to seek nourishment. It is through our personal connection to the Great Life that we begin to be nourished from within. When we are unable to do this, we will seek nourishment from other sources.

Although we cannot simply decide to have inner integrity, we can prepare ourselves by reclaiming our connection to the fundamentals of our faith and recognizing the wisdom that is contained within these traditions. This can then provide the foundation from which we can arise and find our own spiritual path. Some of us may have had our feeling for religion or spirituality colored or tainted by negative experience. As a consequence, we might seek a connection with the Great Life in some other way. Perhaps it is time to take another look at our spiritual foundation in order to get in touch with the wholeness that each of us seeks.

While going back to basics is very important, if we never venture forth from these initial beliefs and ideas our perspectives will remain rather fundamental. This in turn will limit our range of feelings, actions, and sensory awareness. In other words, our map or territory will lack width, and we may view other people, ideas, or models of religion or spirituality through judgmental eyes. As our beliefs become even more firm, unwavering, and unbending, we become inflexible and defensive. This absence of flexibility can give rise to a fundamentalist perspective. Our integrity then becomes a dividing line between those we perceive as the "other" and ourselves, rather than a bridge that connects us. The recent escalation in the number of fundamentalist groups may be attributed to their feeling the need for a stronger religious presence in a modern world where they feel marginalized; they cling to their fundamentalist beliefs as a reaction to what they consider to be the moral disintegration of society.

In fact, the fundamentalist is present in all of us. If we look closely we will probably notice the part of ourselves that strongly adheres to our beliefs, and vigorously defends our position that "this is the way it is." It predisposes us to judge those who challenge or in some way differ from us. As our flexibility begins to unfold, it gives us a width that allows us to expand beyond our initial beliefs and viewpoints and consider other perspectives.

Integrity is the initiating impetus that begins our journey.

In a world predominated by the desire for instant results or gratification, we often seek instant spiritual experiences. These then become what we consider to be our spiritual life. Without integrity or a fundamental connection to our spiritual foundation, however, we may lack the context or framework to understand and integrate what we have experienced into our lives. Integrity not only provides this connection between one's spiritual experience and life, but it also allows us to begin to discriminate between those experiences that come from the Great Life and those that may not.

Integrity is one of several paths. It distinguishes itself from the others because it is the right path, and the only one upon which you will never get lost.

—M.H.McKee

The development of integrity is unique to every individual and depends on how we experience our world. It is often unformed and must develop over time. Some of us may believe we are persons of great integrity, yet in reality we are often only imitating its form—the behaviors, thoughts, and actions that society has accepted as demonstrative of integrity. As we do this, the seeds of its content begin to germinate so that we have an inner understanding of the meaning of true integrity.

Several years ago while living in England, I met a man who had accompanied a patient to my office. He casually mentioned that he had just returned to England after living in New Zealand for the past ten years.

The following week, I was surprised to discover that this same man had scheduled an appointment with me. He stated that upon meeting me the week before, he had suddenly experienced a hot feeling all over his body. It was such a sudden and unusual sensation that he remarked on it at the time to his friend, and decided that he should come and visit me.

The curious thing is that over the preceding six months, I myself had also been experiencing odd, random hot flushes that would engulf my body without explanation. I had jokingly remarked that it must be male menopause, but secretly wondered whether this was the precursor to a heart attack or some other deadly pathophysiology. I decided not to mention this at the time he was relating his story, but listened as the man explained that he had been a member of a Sufi community for the past ten years. The community was headed by a Sheikh and was firmly founded and modeled on Islamic principles. He described the Sheikh as an idealistic, charismatic, and paternalistic man who had enabled him to develop a love and devotion for God. He had learned to surrender through his teacher, who embodied what he felt was a true connection to God. It had appeared to be a beneficial process, but he had of late felt the need to establish his own direct connection to God rather than one that depended upon an intermediary.

While he was telling his story, I again became flushed and hot from head to toe. This man exclaimed that he, too, was having the same experience. We sat together quietly, each of us inwardly asking God to give us an understanding of what we were being shown. After a period of time, we suddenly and almost simultaneously exclaimed that these hot flushes were to signal us that our integrity, our true inner connection to God, was germinating. Our realization was that for years each of us, in our own way, had been preparing the soil for this to happen. At an outer level we had practiced our "uprightness" by honoring the truth when a lie or half truth was preferable, or by clinging to our viewpoints when it would have been more politically correct to go with the flow. We had even become rather rigid in our views and often dogmatic. We had created an upright foundation and followed a straight path with words and prayers. However small, this seed had now germinated within each of us, allow-

ing a much deeper connection to grow. This internal heat, a sympathetic adrenergic rush at a physical level, was seen as a mirror of the spontaneous release of heat that occurs when a seed expands, and changes within, ready to burst forth and sprout.—Solihin

Sometimes we copy or borrow integrity by seeking the assistance of those whom we regard as more elevated than ourselves to facilitate our own connection to the Divine. This may be a teacher, spiritual leader, guide, or guru. In reality, all human beings have the capacity to develop their own direct relationship with God. When we do this we have found our true inner integrity. This provides the support and inner guidance that enables us to know our own truth, eliminating the need to seek answers from external sources. Ultimately, our inner integrity is our unwavering connection to God. It enables us to connect with our inner feelings, our power, humanity, and nobility. This allows our posture and spine to be straight, our feelings to be congruent, our animal nature to be obedient, our humanity to be uncompromising, and our nobility in serving God to be unwavering.

8

The Vegetative Self

I drink of the wine of life,
savoring the breadth of all that it offers
from the majesty of a snow-capped mountain
to the searching touch of a baby's fingers
the wonder of creation moves me,
even from the depths of my darkness and sorrow
my feelings can soar like an eagle high above
the peace and stillness of a forest,
as I yearn to taste the feeling of life within.

An awareness of both our internal and external environments enables humans to taste the full array of delights that life and nature can provide. This is the realm of our senses and feelings, where we process and digest life, and nourish ourselves both inwardly and outwardly. This vegetative life force defines the second level of the life forces hierarchy and is the innate momentum that moved evolution forward to create life from mere matter. Within this animating life force are all the instructions and nuances of the plant (vegetative) kingdom.

The vegetative life force awakens the passion to "taste" life, prompting us to seek ways to feel alive. This rather "greedy" force will urge us to take whatever we need to ensure our survival. It provides the impetus to maintain homeostasis so that we feel good and have a sense of well-being. It is present from the moment of conception, animating our DNA, prompting it to divide and replicate, germinating and nourishing the seeds of our genetic material. Ultimately, this brings alive the feeling of our true potential.

As we take in sensory information, we label and interpret it as a feeling. At the most basic level, our feelings indicate when we are hungry, tired, cold, hot, and other such things. They alert us when danger is near, tell us when we are happy or irritated with someone or something, or let us know when we have been hurt or have hurt someone else. Our sensory awareness is not limited to the known and tangible, but also to that which is unseen. This is why we cannot always explain our feelings.

The feeling nature of a human is very wide and expansive. Our feelings are like plants in a garden, and various events in our lives water them so that they begin to grow. This garden can be filled with lovely and delightful feelings as well as ones that are unpleasant and need to be weeded out. As we tend to our internal environment, weeding, sifting through and turning our feelings, our state is one of balance and harmony. Those of us who maintain a garden will probably see the close parallel between how we maintain it and how we tend to our own feeling nature.

When we moved to our house several years ago, its two acres were completely overgrown with blackberries that were so thick that you could not walk through the property. We have spent much time and effort clearing the land of them, but we left a long hedge of blackberries to enjoy their delicious fruit. A couple of years ago we were so busy with work and travel that our entire blackberry harvest remained unpicked. This felt like a terrible waste to me, and I vowed not to let it happen again.

Last year as the berries started to ripen, I went out every two or three days to pick. As they were picked on a regular basis there were almost no bad ones, only a seemingly endless flow of delicious, juicy blackberries. I also enjoyed the feeling of being out there, usually at the end of the day, for a time of quiet gathering. I developed a rhythm of picking and bringing bowls of berries into the kitchen to make jam or freeze for winter eating. As the rows of shiny, dark purple pots started to fill my storage cupboard, I felt a great sense of joy and satisfaction. It felt so good to be using the resources that we have been given, eating them each day, storing some for later use, and giving jars to friends. This became a metaphor for me, to make better use of my resources in all areas of my life.—Alicia

*In his majestic trilogy **The Lord of the Rings**, Tolkien depicts Ents as sentient tree beings, and introduces the idea that the vegetative kingdom has a remarkable awareness and ability to provide for its survival. This is seen in the real world where plants have the capacity to regenerate, adjust and adapt.*

Our sensory awareness has evolved from the more primitive capabilities of the vegetative (plant) kingdom, hence the name "vegetative life force." Plants have a basic sensory system that monitors and responds to their internal and external environments: turning and growing towards the sun, adapting root growth according to the availability of nutrients, wilting to conserve water, and so forth. This rudimentary but nevertheless sophisticated cellular specialization ensures a plant's survival. In addition, plants have an extraordinary ability to respond and adapt to their external environments. Using its sensory awareness, a plant can initiate and create a strategy for survival at the appropriate moment.

In the vegetative kingdom, the hierarchical arrangement of flora is seen where some species edge out their "competitors," and some thrive in the shadows of others.

In the Sahel region of Africa, some species of acacia trees, the leaves of which are tempting to the desert gazelle, can manufacture toxic and distasteful tannins that render the leaves inedible within minutes of an initial tree being "attacked." In addition, the tree produces a chemical transmitter that is carried via the wind to neighboring trees, who in turn manufacture their own tannins. This same adaptive dynamic is mirrored in our own vegetative system, which allows human physiology to adapt to specific situations. For example, people unaccustomed to going without food will initially feel hungry when deprived, as their bodies urge them to find more food. Within a day or so, however, the body adapts by slowing down physical activity to conserve energy, and the ache of hunger diminishes.

The evolutionary elements of primitive vegetative life are evident in one's own physiology, autonomic nervous system, and senses. These are the differing systems within our bodies that nurture us and provide for our needs by digesting, cleaning, respiring, excreting, and pumping the vital elements that maintain life. The vegetative life force animates these systems, and is constantly monitoring and responding to our internal and external environments to create physiological ease and a feeling of well-being. Even a newborn baby demonstrates the presence of this force as it roots for the nipple in search of food.

When functioning effectively, our neurology is hardwired to monitor and process all sensory input through our autonomic nervous systems (ANS). The ANS clearly demonstrates the duality of life in its two complimentary branches: the sympathetic nervous system (SNS) and the parasympathetic nervous system (PNS). The SNS, often called the fight/flight system, is responsible for energy utilization. This "global spy network" listens to everything, reacting to the slightest signal with a liberal dose of neurotransmitters that evoke a defensive response. In our hectic lives, the SNS is usually "on" most of the time, so we are always preparing for action. This depletes our reserves, exhausts us, and creates the all-too-familiar feeling of stress.

In contrast to the SNS, the PNS is responsible for energy conservation. It resets the "pumped up" nature of the systems of the body that have been altered by the SNS, and thus prepares us for rest, repair, and digestion. It regulates the organs and glands that assimilate, process, and eliminate what we take in.

By ensuring that we sweat to keep our internal heat down, and urinate and defecate to void waste and excess fluid, the ANS maintains a balanced internal environment conducive to action and work that is critical to our survival. A physiology that cannot adapt to a changing environment is an indication that basic housekeeping mechanisms are not functioning properly. Our cellular environment then becomes toxic and we begin to feel unwell.

We interact with our environment through our senses of smell, taste, touch, sight, and hearing, which constantly supply us with an abundance of information. These senses are very sophisticated adaptations of the rudimentary plant "sense," a necessity for survival in a predatory world. Our feelings arise from the interpretation of these sensory stimuli, which may be generated from either an internal or external source.

Touch is one sense that is vital to our survival. Babies who are not held and touched do not thrive, even when all their other needs are met. This has been documented in hospitals in which premature babies spent all their time isolated in incubators. When volunteers began to massage, stroke and hold the babies, however, the infants grew faster, and were more alert and active than babies who lacked such contact. Throughout our lives, this contact is essential for us to feel "in touch" with others as well as with ourselves. Those who are not surrounded by close friends or extended family can feel isolated and alone without this essential contact and nourishment. One study found that elderly ladies who went to the hair salon each week to have their hair washed and set tended to do so simply because they craved physical contact.

Our sensory capacity is the interface between our feelings and the external world. Sometimes we have difficulty processing something we have taken in. Just as we might get indigestion after a heavy meal, a *feeling* that we are unable to handle or "digest" can also make us feel sick. When we suspect that this has happened, it is important to try and understand the source of those feelings so we can address them.

On either side of the river, is the tree of life...and the leaves of the tree are for healing of the nations.
—The Book of Revelations
22:2

> *In 1998 my husband Peter and I planned a trip to the Indonesian island of Bali. Our plans included bringing our three teenage children, who had never traveled abroad. The day before our departure, our daughter Martha came to me complaining that she felt sick. Despite my assurances that nothing was wrong, she left the room only to return a few minutes later complaining that she now felt even worse. This time, I suggested we both surrender and ask to be shown what was really going on with her. As I became quiet, I suddenly recalled that when I had first mentioned the trip some six months prior, Martha expressed a great fear of flying, and said she did not want to go.*

| 59 |

When we finished surrendering, I asked her to visualize herself on the plane bound for Bali. Her broad smile indicated that we had located an important piece of information. I reminded her that her initial lack of enthusiasm about going to Bali might be related to her current malaise. Moreover, I suggested that perhaps it was not so much a fear of airplanes and flying, but rather a reluctance to venture into new territory that was responsible for her queasiness.

With that realization, her "illness" instantly disappeared. In the space of fifteen minutes, she had gone from hanging her head over the bathroom sink to inhaling a sandwich on her way out the door. Two months after the trip, I became aware that despite two thirteen-hour flights and four plane changes, Martha never once expressed any further concern about flying. Embracing the opportunity to move beyond anything she had ever done enabled her to avoid being held by her own fear of new adventures. It had been a pivotal moment for our daughter. Two years later she would accompany me on a trip to India and subsequently become an exchange student in Europe.—Alexandra

Everyone responds to external forces in their own unique way. For example, a piece of art might leave one person feeling uplifted and inspired, but evoke a feeling of distaste or disinterest in another. Sometimes several people who experience the same event each have a very different feeling or memory associated with it. A recent workshop included a man who expressed a powerful sentiment towards the rest of the group. In response to his statement, a woman participant said that "everyone" was feeling threatened by this man. In fact, when questioned, not one other person in the group agreed with her. It was important for the woman who had made this statement, and for all of us, to recognize that when we feel something, however strongly, it does not necessarily mean that others share the same feeling.

A friend and I were visiting the Holocaust Museum in Washington, D.C. I had heard a lot about it and knew that the museum was designed to give visitors a sense of the atrocities of the holocaust, so that it is never forgotten. We entered the museum with a slight feeling of trepidation. We bought our tickets in the foyer and stepped into the elevator which would take us to the upper floors where the main part of the museum

was located. In the elevator were a number of other people. It began to move, but after a few moments we came to a standstill, and the doors did not open. As I looked around I could see the faces of some people becoming tense and anxious. My friend confided that she was starting to get worried about being stuck and was feeling claustrophobic. I, feeling unconcerned, commented that maybe this was intentional; that they were introducing us to the feeling of what it was like to be trapped in a metal box like the trains that transported the Jews to the concentration camps. Her response was "They wouldn't be allowed to do that!"

Although several people in the elevator were becoming very anxious, I felt quite calm and was not worried. A few moments later we started to move downwards again. When the doors opened, very apologetic museum staff were waiting to meet us. They explained that the elevator had malfunctioned. They added that this had never happened before. Some of the people who had been in the elevator then chose to walk up the stairs rather than take another elevator. Again, we reacted differently according to our interpretation of the experience and what feelings that brought up in each of us in relation to our own personal histories.—Alicia

Why the variety of responses? The answer lies in the limbic system, the part of the brain that takes in and collates information from a variety of sources. This emotional memory bank consists of our own repertoire of life experiences as well as our familial histories. It recalls and equates the current situation with what it has already experienced and then labels it. The resulting feelings and emotions are often tempered and colored by events that occurred long ago. When our feelings are based on old, outdated, or habitual memory, they can improperly affect how we respond to the present situation. It is as if we are viewing the present through the eyes of the past. By becoming more aware of your feeling state, you can begin to differentiate between an old feeling or memory and a feeling that is actually justified in the present moment. In other words, is the feeling relevant to this situation, or is it perhaps something you have called up from your past?

Through our sense of smell we have an incredible capacity to access memories. This olfactory history is stored deep within the limbic brain. This is why a smell can instantaneously bring old and long-forgotten feelings into the present.

Being Human

Our feelings are often based on the past rather than the present.

Smell is a potent wizard that transports us across thousands of miles and all the years we have lived. The odors of fruits waft me to my southern home, to my childhood frolics in the peach orchard. Other odors, instantaneous and fleeting, cause my heart to dilate joyously or contract with remembered grief.
—Helen Keller

Years ago we had a new carpet installed. It had a rubber underlay, which, for the first few days, had a strong rubbery smell. I started to feel very anxious and nauseous, and couldn't understand why, until I suddenly realized that the smell reminded me of the rubber gas mask at the dentist! As a child, I had been given anesthesia a few times and all the feelings I was now having were associated with the fear I felt as a child, as the mask was placed over my face. Once I recognized this, those feelings completely disappeared.

(As I finished writing this, my son came in and told me how the perfume of a woman he had sat next to on the bus today reminded him of our visit to the Viking Museum in York, England, thirteen years ago! It was an interesting coincidence, as he had no idea what I had been writing about!)—Alicia

Because the vegetative life force strives to maintain and nourish us, it serves as our provider. The provider is like a maid, cook, and maintenance person all rolled into one. In the most rudimentary sense, it is this force that prompts us to take action to provide for ourselves, but its actions are seldom limited to our own personal needs. Many of us are quite familiar with juggling the demands of family and career in order to provide for others. In fact, for some of us, the provider is so well honed that we provide for the needs of others at our own expense. This may be an unproductive attempt to bolster or validate our own feeling of value.

Growing up as the oldest daughter of a large family I was used to taking care of others and being "responsible." The women in my family were all capable caregivers—my paternal grandmother was widowed at a young age and had to raise four children alone.

As I grew older, I often found it easier to provide for others than for myself. As a result of not taking care of my own needs for nourishment and rest I would sometimes burn out. There was also an element of providing for others so that I would feel of value. I still like to do things for others, but no longer at my own expense. I also recognized that sometimes when we take care of something for someone else, we can actually prevent them from utilizing their own resources, so we may not actually be serving their needs either.—Alicia

The homes in which we live reveal an enormous amount about our provider. Because this is where we go to drop our workday persona, many of us try to create an environment conducive to replenishing and nurturing ourselves. How we arrange, care for and live in our homes, whether they are cluttered or orderly, dark or light, gloomy or open all reflect something about how we provide for ourselves. *How* we live in our houses is also important. Consider how a house that is host to arguments, discord, or tension provides an entirely different atmosphere for its occupants than one that contains more balanced and loving interactions.

While most of us are very aware of our own feeling natures, what may be less obvious is how often the force of our feelings colors everything we do. When our feelings take power we have surrendered to them, and consequently all our actions, thoughts, and choices are dictated by or mediated through them. One example of this is when we feel unsupported. When this feeling prevails, we often point an accusatory finger at those around us, decrying their words and actions as "unsupportive." While this may be justified in some cases, most of the time it reflects a lack of support from within us, rather than on the part of those around us. If the force of our feelings swamps us, we are operating from a feeling-based reality in which that which is not real "feels" real. Our neurotransmitters, which handle the expression of sensation, are "tripped" all the time, so our feelings overwhelm and entangle us, like the vines in a jungle. At that moment, our feelings are running the show.

Several years ago, a Zambian woman came to see me in London. She was from a large family, and most of her siblings were stricken with AIDS or were HIV positive. Despite a life free of casual or unprotected sex, she was fearful and despondent, terrified of the possibility of contracting a disease that had become the scourge of equatorial Africa. As we worked together, it became apparent that her feelings of malaise regarding both her family and that of her country had overwhelmed her.

When I suggested that her feelings had entangled her, somewhat like a vine, she gasped audibly. She then said that her family's home was actually overgrown and enclosed by vines. She realized how the vines mirrored her own "overgrown" feelings of fear, which had become dominant. Upon

her return home, she cut the vines down. She later told me she felt a free-
dom in her life that she had not been able to previously sense.—Solihin

One of the most important aspects of the vegetative life force is the way in which we are nourished by it. In the external world we might initially associate this nourishing force only with things derived from the vegetative (plant) kingdom, such as food, drink, drugs, tobacco, and alcohol. In reality, anything that changes our feeling state—music, art, clothing, sex, or other forms of intimate body contact—contains a vegetative life force that nourishes us. Consider, for example, a walk in the countryside, where the beauty of nature in the verdant mountains, hills, grass, shrubs, and trees can dramatically shift our feeling state. Human actions can also demonstrate a nourishing force in the form of a kind word, a soothing hand, a broad smile, or a gentle glance, each of which uplifts the recipient.

Just as food represents sustenance for our outer animal body, the feelings are the nourishment for our inner animal nature.

Although we can be nourished in a variety of ways, the word "nourishment" is usually associated with food. Within an individual's vegetative life force is carried information about nourishment that is specific to a particular culture. For example, the way a Tibetan is nourished—through environment, clan, and food—is different from that of someone who is American or Japanese. The way in which we nourish ourselves originates from our culture and genetic coding and is reinforced in our home environment. Our parents' behaviors, mannerisms, etiquette, and dynamics of eating become our initial mode of consciousness. Likewise, as children we copy the attitudes and choices made by our peers with regard to eating. These cultural variations get seeded and watered day in, day out, and they determine how we nourish ourselves.

In all cultures, sharing food is an essential part of most celebrations. The rituals associated with eating—the preparation of the food and table, the washing of hands and saying a prayer—are universal. When we savor our food, our company, and our environment, we are being nourished in many ways. In recent years, the broader concept of nourishment has taken a back seat to mere sustenance as we allocate less and less time to relax, enjoy, and assimilate what we have ingested. Many meals are eaten on the run; the myriad number of fast-food restaurants that pepper the American landscape attest that this is a nation of people who eat while driving. With the advent of microwave ovens, we have spawned a new generation of children who prepare entire meals from a box in less than five minutes. In addition, many of us feel the need to constantly eat, drink, nibble, or chew, even when we are busy doing something else. All of this overloads our digestive system, leaving no room to process and digest our food or other aspects of our life.

Today's rushed lifestyle prompts certain questions about our eating habits. How often do we sit down for a leisurely meal, whether at home or at a restaurant? Are we hurried and stressed, hardly noticing what we are eating, or are we relaxed, appreciating how the food looks, smells, and tastes? Do we take a moment of quiet before a meal to express our gratitude for what we are receiving? Do we open our homes to others, or share a meal that we have prepared with them? Far too often we focus too much on *what* we eat, without giving equal attention to *how* we eat.

External environments also nourish us, and are particular to personal preference. For example, the quiet and natural beauty of the countryside nourishes some people, while others need the noise and action of a busy city. Our preferences are often dictated not so much by the physical surroundings themselves, but by our experiences in those surroundings.

> As a child I lived a rather dual and segmented life, between the deserts of Kuwait and boarding school in the lush beauty of the Scottish Highlands. I now live in Oregon, where the climate is similar to Scotland. Occasionally the continual rain and the inclement weather pulls up memories of school life, and of an ancient and green Scotland. Despite its physical beauty, my recollections of school and my years in Scotland do not nourish me. Instead, I recall an (academic) environment that was harsh, unkind, and filled with an old and ancient lack of vibrancy, as well as a sort of "caste system" that stifled, choked, and enslaved us, and challenged our ancestral loyalties.
>
> In contrast, a wide and open desert environment takes me back to my childhood feelings of the wonder and beauty hidden in the apparent emptiness of a desert. I spent a large amount of time in this hot and arid yet dynamic environment. It was there that I learned how to be quiet; the silence of the desert emphasized my own silence. In this seemingly

barren land, the potential for life is always present. This environment nourished me, and whenever I am in a similar place I instantly feel replete and at home.—Solihin

Sometimes we confuse a hunger for something other than food with a need to ingest more food. This is often the case with those who consume any substance in an attempt to fill a hole created by, or insulate themselves from, their feelings of anger, pain, inadequacy, or other uncomfortable feelings.

I've had a love/hate relationship with food for most of my life, ranging from adhering to a strict "healthy" diet to midnight food forays that would put to shame even the most notorious of gluttons. In addition, over the last few years, I noticed that anytime I needed to write something yet was unclear about what to say, or whether what I was trying to communicate would be of any interest to anyone, I would invariably develop a sudden "hunger" and steer myself to the refrigerator.

I have shared my eating woes with many other people, some of whom have experienced a similar desire to eat when faced with a stressful, difficult, or unknown situation. It wasn't until the last few months of writing this book that I discovered that the times when I most craved some form of external nourishment were the times when I felt the least connected to myself—to the core of who I am. Whenever this happens, I no longer feel nourished from within, from all the parts of me that should serve me as I write, speak, and interact with others. Instead, what takes power is a feeling of worthlessness, of failure, of my inability to offer anything of value to anyone, and least of all to myself.

I believe that my hunger is created by my need to satiate this huge, dark loneliness, the force of which orchestrates my temporary meltdown. In a country plagued by a growing problem with obesity, I cannot help but think that others may also experience something similar. Is our battle of the bulge really handled by calorie/fat/fiber/ carbo counting, or do we perhaps need to focus more on how we are nourished from the inside out, rather than solely from the outside in?—Alexandra

When we lead hectic and busy lives, we are bombarded with huge amounts of extraneous data as well as important information. If we do not know how to cull out only the information that we need, we may become overloaded with input, and hence, overwhelmed by feelings, either good or bad. Just as we can nourish ourselves poorly by eating junk food, we are inadequately nourished by poisoned or toxic feelings. Feelings such as anger, worthlessness, sadness, and despair can take power when they are not cleaned or released, and they color and affect our interactions with others. The inability to properly process and clean our feelings will eventually manifest in our physical bodies as digestive problems, lethargy, exhaustion, bad breath, body odor, skin problems, nausea, or, in extreme cases, poor immune function, constipation, or an irritated bowel.

Our body contains a fairly sophisticated neural architecture known in western physiology as *plexi*. These plexi are bundles of nerves that are interconnected and serve as the "mini brains" or processors of the autonomic nervous system. They form a housekeeping mechanism that registers and makes simple reflexive and autonomic responses to input.

Thousands of years ago eastern philosopher-priests were able to intuit or "see" the flow of different energies—which we would call the forces. They constructed a map of these seven interconnected plexi which became what we now know as the *chakra* system. As they didn't have an anatomical perspective, this system became interwoven with their map of spirituality. The two cultural models—east and west—have now come together as we integrate the idea of the association of energy centers with the workings of the plexi.

When we are unable to tune into the Great Life we often seek other avenues or outlets to nourish us.

Within the plexi/chakras, neurotransmitters trigger the flow of electrons, which creates an electromagnetic field. These fields then accumulate "debris," sensations, and feelings that have a "charge." When we fail to let go of these accumulations, or charges, the body becomes overwhelmed. When we retain old emotions, feelings, and sensations within the chakras, our "house" becomes "dirty," or at the very least, full of old stuff. The chakras function as a housecleaning mechanism to ensure that we do not operate off old sensations, feelings, and memories. When functioning properly, they are automatic, discharging on their own. Unfortunately, the human mind can impede this process by continually remembering, rehashing, and rethinking old feelings. When this happens it interferes with the cleaning process. If we get our heads out of the way, our chakras can function effectively.

It is the provider's job to clean our human house, which includes clearing away any feelings and emotions that no longer serve us. Most of us can recall a situation in which we did not express what we truly felt, only to later regret our silence. As these unexpressed feelings build up inside us, they are stored as emotions. If we carry emotional wounds they will color our feelings and affect the way we relate to others. A memory or some other event will often trigger a response in which we release these stored feelings. These emotional outbursts reflect our inability to contain them any longer.

In extreme cases, being "nourished" by unpleasant feelings can lead to addictions such as drugs, alcohol, shopping, television, gambling, food, and sex as we attempt to alter or mask our feeling state.

We have each devised our own ways of shifting our emotional states when we don't like how we feel. Some might drink a glass of wine. Others may smoke, have sex, exercise, or watch television. These activities all change our physiology, which in turn changes our chemistry. The end result is that we feel different, but that is only part of the story. Rather than dealing with unpleasant or difficult feelings, we often use these means to stimulate our senses to shift state. When we merely skim the surface by doing something that changes how we feel in the present moment, we fail to address the original source of our feelings.

Men and women tend to have very different ways of processing feelings and recording information. While men remember an event, women remember the feeling associated with it.

How do we clean our feelings? Sometimes we can simply decide to let them go, or we can express them verbally and take action on them. Often we can make a conscious choice to become bigger than the force of our feelings. If a particular feeling is too large or too familiar, and we recognize that it is often present or in power, we can offer it up in our prayers or surrender. The capacity to forgive ourselves and others is what allows for the healing of these emotional wounds. By letting go of feelings that are old or no longer useful, you create a space inside yourself for something new to develop.

When we are connected to the Great Life force, we can begin to clear away feelings that no longer serve us. This is when our integrity can bring us back into homeostasis and balance so that we are able to face our feelings, and sort through, discriminate, and recognize what we need and what is no longer required. Without integrity, it can be very difficult for us to gauge how we really feel, and thus we can be easily led astray by following all sorts of feelings, even ones that may feel very "right," as feelings can be very seductive.

The cultural overtones carried by the vegetative life force are what make each human unique, and each tribe and nation as well. Common to all humanity, however, is the desire to be in the flow of the essence of that which truly nourishes—the Great Life. Sometimes we still feel disconnected and separate from others, reality, the Great Life, or even ourselves. We may have a feeling that something is missing, or have some longing inside that quietly yet relentlessly prompts us to seek a deeper connection through which we can feel truly alive—one that allows life and others to "touch" us. It is only when we are aligned with this central unifying force that we can taste what is real. This connection gives rise to our *inner feelings*, which represent a truth irrespective of our cultural, racial, and other differences. Inner feelings are not the result of the interpretation of sensory stimuli. Instead, they represent a clarity from deep within that brings alive a connection to our truth and ourselves that supports and nourishes us.

By reclaiming our connection to the Great Life, we can regain the sense that we contain everything we need to feel supported in our lives.

True inner feelings are pristine: they are not altered or changed in response to external stimuli.

9

Flexibility

I no longer fear that which I cannot comprehend
As I quietly journey beyond the
protective boundaries of my mind
my heart begins to dance when
almost imperceptibly
the movement of life begins
to spiral throughout my being

The board game "Snakes and Ladders" challenges players to be the first to advance to the winning square by moving along a set pathway. Landing on a snake along the way sends the player backwards or sideways, while landing on a ladder allows the player to vertically move closer to the final square. The game is thought to have originated in India and was perhaps, like many games, a way to teach at an unconscious level the simple idea that a ladder (integrity) can bridge things or lead us towards our destination, and that a snake (flexibility) can be dangerous, and can lead us astray.

The image of a snake is used to symbolize flexibility, the second essential human quality. Throughout history, the symbol of the snake has been associated with an enormous range of qualities, from wholeness, wisdom, transformation, and movement to life and death. Its dual nature is evident in that some cultures fear the snake as evil, seductive, and poisonous, while others revere it as a symbol of life, fertility, wisdom, and wholeness. Common to all these interpretations is that the snake is seen as transformative—whether giving life or taking it away. This quality is demonstrated in the story of Medusa, whose hair of writhing snakes caused those who set eyes upon her to be transformed into stone. Today's European pharmacies use a symbol that acknowledges this transformational quality: a goblet, entwined by a snake whose venom drops into the vessel, implying that even the poison of the snake can be transformed into the elixir of health.

Flexibility represents our ability to transform by shedding that which is no longer needed.

The snake rising up the central axis illustrates how the presence of integrity guides our flexibility so that our thoughts and actions are tempered by integrity. In its most basic interpretation, the flexible form of the snake wrapped around the staff signifies our capacity to "move" in response to sensory stimuli. The spiral-shaped symbol of the snake ascending the staff is mirrored throughout nature, from the double helix of our chromosomal DNA to the spiraled chambers of the shell of a nautilus. Spirals are also seen in such elemental forces as tornadoes, the star nebulae of the Milky Way, and even the way water drains from our bath. The spiral embodies the qualities of flexibility—movement and evolution, the rhythm within all things, and a widening and expanding of life.

Flexibility provides a pathway for feelings and sensations to arise. These are then interpreted by the animal self, which reacts accordingly. This transforms our state from one of inaction to action. For this reason, flexibility is the bridge between the vegetative and animal levels of the life forces hierarchy.

It is the innate resource of flexibility that keeps us in step with the rhythm of life. When we are out of step with this rhythm we are unable to connect with the feeling of being alive. When our cellular mechanisms, our physiology, and the intimate workings of our body are in rhythm with the various cycles, they keep us in balance and repair. In a broader sense, we also need to be in rhythm with our world—in harmony with the seasons, with the days and nights, with our families and partners. The need to be a harmonious note in the wondrous melody of life makes many of us do our best to be in tune with our families, communities, and world. When modern life compels us to work out of synch with our natural rhythms, however, we often adapt to this imposed regimen so that we can conform to the niche or identity we have built for ourselves. As a result, our internal clocks begin to alter and we lose the dynamic equilibrium—our own inner rhythm—that connects us to ourselves.

The loss of our connection to our own inner rhythm can be a precursor to illness. When we become ill and out of sorts, it is because we have become stagnant and static, out of step with the movement of life. Our physiology becomes impaired, and we begin to illustrate this with altered chemistry and less energy. The grin goes away, the laughter subsides, and our joie de vivre wanes. If we are unable to move beyond this state it becomes chronic, and we continually "sit in our own stuff." It is as if the snake, our flexibility, wanders around in our "house" but is unable to climb up and provide the means to move out of or beyond our stuck state. Sometimes we attempt to ascend from a stuck state by using a "sidewinder" approach. This only moves us laterally, however; it does not address or change the underlying problem. Although this approach demonstrates flexibility, it is flexibility in the absence of integrity. Flexibility can only serve us effectively when it is accompanied by integrity, enabling us to rise up and take action to change the situation.

Many of us find it difficult to take action on our feelings. Perhaps we don't like dealing with them, or perhaps our familial pattern is to sweep things

When two snakes are entwined or coupled in conjugation, they mirror the double helix of the DNA strands in our chromosomes, or the representation of the chakras in ancient Hindu texts and pictures.

In some South American shamanic practices a snakelike vine produces a potent hallucinatory chemical used for religious rites and vision quests.

under the carpet; it may be culturally taboo to express feelings, or we may simply not be attentive of them. Regardless of the reasons, we often hold on to feelings rather than deal with, face, or process them. When we are unable to exclaim, grouse, or react, these feelings become bottled up. They carry a charge, and without the flexibility needed to take action and discharge them, their emotional debris fills us. This affects our physiology, which in turn alters all our other components—our posture and stance, protective mechanisms, immune system and even our interpretation of what we are experiencing.

Without flexibility we remain held by past experiences with no ability to move beyond them.

As we age, or perhaps lose touch with the feeling of life, our tendency to become more rigid and inflexible increases. Certainly, for some of us, it is true that we need to develop the capacity to bend a bit more. This is evident in those who rigidly cling to their beliefs, fears, and habits. If we can reconnect with our capacity to be flexible, however, we can then widen and expand these narrow viewpoints to be inclusive rather than exclusive without compromising our integrity.

On New Year's Eve in 1996, my husband Peter and I sat together and evaluated how our lives had changed over the course of the year. One year earlier we had been introduced to the idea of the life forces. Since that time, I had recognized that my rigidity of thought had been incredibly limiting to both me and my family.

At some point that evening, Peter mentioned that he would like to explore the possibility of moving to California to advance his career. This had been a familiar topic over the years, and each time he had broached the subject it was always met with a resounding "NO!" from me. To his surprise, this time I agreed and said that I would support that effort. The doorway had swung open, and a new chapter in our lives was about to be written.

Three weeks later, Peter announced that he had been offered an incredible opportunity in Los Angeles. In the next four weeks we sold our Atlanta house, bought our Los Angeles house, and moved our family from one coast to another. Now, more than five years later, we are all absolutely convinced that it was the wisest decision we ever made.

Developing flexibility is a little like doing yoga exercises that challenge you to bend in a certain posture, and then repeat the posture and bend even more. Just when you thought you'd reached your limit on the first go-round, you reach inside and find the part of you that takes you even further. Our move to California had done just that—it allowed us to widen our perspectives and viewpoints beyond all that we had previously known. And thankfully so, because during the writing of this book we moved again—this time back across the country. This move was also accomplished with the same relative ease, in large measure because, by being flexible, we were able to recognize and act on opportunities that otherwise would have been missed.—Alexandra

Just as some people are not flexible enough, others can be too flexible. Those who are willing to do anything to maintain the status quo demonstrate this by bending to accommodate others, often at their own expense. Those with extremely flexible minds enjoy the virtue of enormous creativity, but they can also misuse this resource to craft language that is confusing to others in an attempt to mask inappropriate actions or avoid telling the truth. If we become too flexible—too wide and indiscriminate—in our thoughts, feelings, and actions, we may end up going down a potentially destructive path. Taken to an extreme, we can lose touch with reality and spiral out of control because we lack the boundaries (integrity) within which to contain ourselves.

Throughout history, the symbol of the snake has been both revered as an icon of wisdom and healing and feared as the tempter of Adam and Eve. In the context of the life forces, we might interpret their story thus: If the vegetation in the Garden of Eden is symbolic of our feeling nature, then the fullness and spread of the branches of the apple tree illustrate the width of our feelings. Although Adam and Eve were forbidden from eating the fruit of the Tree of Knowledge of Good and Evil (duality), the snake tempted Eve, seducing her into tasting the fruit of her feelings. Perhaps this story reminds us of the danger of flexibility in the absence of integrity: Eve's decision to act against the word of God shows her loss of connection (integrity) to the Divine force. When Adam also defied God's order, the two were forever banished from the Garden. Although they had tasted the width of their feelings, they did so with great consequence.

Many cultures recognize the danger of flexibility in the absence of integrity and use moral, civil, and religious injunctions in an attempt to keep people from tasting various "forbidden fruits." These rules are designed to keep order, prevent chaos, and ensure that we stay on the "straight path" in order to contain any errant feelings. They attempt to prevent us from going beyond established boundary lines and into the unknown, because of the recognition that the width of our unbridled feelings can get us into trouble. While these external directives are beneficial in some cases, they can limit us when it may be appropriate to widen or expand our feelings.

An archetype is an inherited pattern of thought or symbolic imagery that originates from the past collective experience and yet is present in our own individual unconscious. All archetypes contain a force, as they embody the ideas, content, and history with which we resonate. Despite the fact that we may not be aware of them at a conscious level, archetypes subtly predispose us to think, feel, or act in particular ways.

The snake is symbolic of our ability to come alive—that is, to taste the enormous range of our feelings and hence engage with the fullness and width of life. Those of us of Judeo-Christian heritage, however, may also carry an embedded archetype of the snake as dangerous and untrustworthy. This mandate against embracing our own flexible nature may prevent us from experiencing a real feeling of being alive. In truth, it is only potentially dangerous to taste forbidden fruit if we do not have integrity. Integrity prevents our feelings from veering off on some errant pathway by always bringing us back to our center. Without it, we may be tempted to act inappropriately on our feelings.

Many years ago, I had a deeply powerful experience in Sri Lanka. The island is rich, verdant, and lush. Its primal vegetative nature touched me so deeply that simply being there nourished me.

I was studying acupuncture there at the Colombo Hospital. We would learn in the morning, practice in the afternoon, and have fun and study in the evenings. I had teamed up with a nurse from New Zealand. She and I would go to a communal study house in the late afternoons to memorize Chinese names and the acupuncture meridian descriptions. After a month of study, we spent more time together as we prepared for our final assessment. We spent much time discussing our understanding of the new work and many other things, and my feelings towards this woman began to grow. Nothing was said, and yet in my head a busy voice kept talking.

Over the next few days, the constant refrain continued in my head. My struggle with the proverbial saint on one shoulder and devil on the other felt unbearable. I would get up, and without uttering a word, go into the walled garden and surrender to God, asking for help and guidance in lift-

ing this conflict. My passion would depart, and I would casually go back in and resume writing or reading. A little while later, I would again be aroused, only to excuse myself and return to the garden to go through the same petition. This scene was repeated over several days until suddenly, it was if all my passions evaporated. The feeling was completely gone.

Although we had never openly expressed any desire for one another, perhaps a knowing smile or fleeting glance had told the hidden story. But I never confided to her the battle that I had fought with myself. The course ended, we all passed, and we said our farewells easily and comfortably. Simply put, I had been off track. However, some part of me was directed to a higher authority, to ask for help when tempted. Thanks be to God that I was able to clean those errant feelings, which left no residue within me. They were transitory, created by the environment and the circumstances, with no substance or reality. —Solihin

The union of integrity and flexibility allows for a transformative experience appropriate to our inner needs, rather than something that is merely transitory, sensational, or a momentary distraction. The quality of integrity is more masculine in nature—upright, present, direct, and penetrating, while flexibility has more feminine qualities—wide, enveloping, fluid, and receptive. We all contain both masculine and feminine aspects. When these two qualities are in balance, we are able to be flexible while remaining grounded.

How do we become more flexible? Initially we can practice giving way, doing things we have never done before, being open to new ideas, and letting go of the old, all of which widen our map. As our flexibility develops, our capacity to see the dual aspect of things, or both sides of the coin, increases. Slowly, this openness allows us to let go of or transform the old beliefs, archetypes, fears, and habits that prevent us from coming alive. When our awareness and consciousness widens, it can change our state and ultimately provide the wherewithal to forge new pathways in both action and thought.

As we come into step with the rhythm of life, we also begin to come alive at an inner level. Our connection with the primary life force is then amplified, and brings into our awareness a vibration, or inner movement. This vibration sustains and nourishes us, cleaning away that which occludes our inner feelings. Historically, people have sought to come alive through experiences, rituals, spiritual techniques, initiations, teachers, and many other means. Perhaps the human quest to find a way to facilitate this awakening, spontaneous movement, or other evidence of a connection to the One is driven by a desire to feel this inner movement. In its presence, all the other forces align in their rightful place with the primary force, and we are reminded with certainty and faith that we are an integral part of life.

10

The Animal Self

ears pricked
the sheen of sweat
across a furrowed brow
eyes nervously scan
nostrils flared
the scent
oh the scent
ah, beauty doth come

Humans have had a relationship with animals since the dawn of time. This relationship has evolved from that of predator and prey to one that is much more complex. We have depended on them for our survival in many ways, whether eating them for sustenance, using them to work for us, or sacrificing them in religious rites. Some spiritual traditions revere animals as aspects of the Divine. In modern times humans have made animals their close companions. This relationship reveals something about our own animal nature. Despite the seemingly vast differences between animals and humans, our genetic information and instructions differ by less than four percent from that of the chimpanzee, our closest relative. Its ability to stand on two feet, to communicate needs and wants, to create social groups, to wage war and to fashion primitive tools bears a striking resemblance to our own human behavior. Both chimpanzees and humans resonate with an innate animal capacity to survive and face the challenges of life.

While traveling through Rajasthan in northwest India, I spent a few days at the Pushkar Camel Fair. This is an incredible event that happens each year in conjunction with an important Hindu festival that is held at the same time. Tens of thousands of camels are herded from all over northern Rajasthan to the outskirts of the holy city of Pushkar.

Very early one morning, I climbed up to a temple set high on a hill above the city. From that vantage point I could see the long lines of camels moving towards the fair. I spent hours just walking through the encampment adjacent to the fair, which was set up in a desert area outside the town. The men sat in groups, dressed in white, with brightly colored turbans and gold earrings, drinking chai and admiring each other's livestock. The women were dressed in pinks, greens, oranges, reds, and golds, with arms covered in jangling bangles.

I watched as the men prepared their camels for display, for races, and for trade, by painting their faces, and sometimes designs on their bod-

ies, or shaving them in intricate patterns, and placing colorfully decorated bridles on them. At one point I heard a dreadful loud groaning and men's voices coming from behind a dune. There, I found a group of men surrounding a camel that was lying on its side in the sand. It had broken its leg and was obviously in great pain. The men all helped to hold the camel still, while two older men attempted to apply a splint to the camel's leg with a wad of herbs and some pieces of wood.

Later still, I watched groups of women carrying huge bundles of green fodder on their heads which they had gathered for their camels. Another woman with a shovel was collecting camel dung and laying it out to dry in the sun. That evening, I saw women cooking on fires that were fueled by the bricks of dried dung. I realized what an integral part of their culture the camel is. Although the camel can survive in the wild, once it has been taken into the service of man it becomes dependent on him for its survival, just as man is dependent on the camel for the survival of this particular culture.—Alicia

Some Native American tribes honored the qualities of certain animals by erecting totem poles to illustrate their close affinity with these animal spirits.

Each of us contains an animal nature, within which is the animal life force. This force represents the third level of the life forces hierarchy. In fact, hierarchical systems are the norm in the animal kingdom where, unlike the vegetative realm, there are pecking orders, alpha males and females, a food chain, and other such systems. The animal life force serves as the guardian of our human house. Its job is to be attentive to and serve its human master. It manifests as our power: our capacity to move and to work, as our strength, sexuality, attractiveness, and territoriality, and as our defensive and protective mechanisms. It is the force that motivates us to rise to the challenge, to be ambitious, and to survive adverse conditions, so that we are not easily pushed around, discounted, or devoured by a bigger animal. It allows us to conceive of and give birth to something new, take action on our feelings, engage with others, and face life in good times and bad.

Hierarchies exist in all kingdoms, but are most obvious in the predator/prey dynamic of the animal realm.

People with type-A personalities are driven by their animal force so they always appear to be "on the go."

If this force becomes dominant we will assume an identity that is based on power, attraction, reaction, habit, sexuality, and ambition. We may be easily sidetracked, tempted to stray and drawn to greener pastures. In addition, we may be so "on-guard" that we neither allow anything new to enter nor allow ourselves to release that which we no longer need.

It is easy to see what we might regard as animal behavior and characteristics in others—the raised voices of two people during an argument, the mother who stops at nothing to protect her child, the athlete who galvanizes every ounce of strength to set a new record, the attractive woman who turns heads, or the charisma of a public figure. We also see it in when someone exerts his or her will and dominance over others to become the "leader of the pack." Yet for some people, the idea of the human animal remains an existential one. We know that we share many similarities with animals—we walk, run, forage, play, and have sexual needs—but we nevertheless "draw the line" to differentiate ourselves from them. The model of the life forces simply indicates that we carry within us the nuances of the animal kingdom, and that these animal forces dictate and influence us in many ways.

The ability to access our animal force is quite useful. A man in one of our workshops experienced his animal nature as a lion. Some time later he was in another workshop. The participants were asked to do an exercise in which one person had to stand in the middle of a room and prevent others from passing by without physical contact. He was chosen for the task and simply allowed the feeling of the lion to arise and be present in him. Not one person passed by him. Afterwards, the other participants wanted to know what he had done, as none of them felt brave enough to challenge him!

Our bodies display an enormous amount of information about the animal life force. We can look at someone's physique, the way they carry their body, and the state of their health and note the strength of their animal force. A person with a spring in their step whose body enables them to actively play sports, and work hard, and who is driven by ambition demonstrates a robust animal force; one who limps along, whose posture slumps, and who lacks energy indicates a weakened or exhausted animal.

Our many animal qualities motivate and support us throughout our lives. They are determined by our genetic predispositions, and they can change and develop according to our individual life circumstances. Our animal aspect is the "nose" of us—the part that sniffs out a good deal, a suitable mate, trouble around the corner, and other such opportunities and challenges. It is the part of all humans that is flighty, selfish, unpredictable, and reactive. These animal qualities enable us to be surefooted, sly like a fox, to carry huge burdens like a pack animal, and to fight and defend ourselves against others. At times, particularly when we feel threatened, we can use these qualities to rise to the occasion. We can stand absolutely still and remain unseen in the face of danger, go on the offensive, or lie low when things heat up. We can slink away in defeat, display our colors and plumage to make an impression, or stand our ground in order to defend our territory.

> *In the late eighties, we taught a workshop in London that included several women who were either actively undergoing treatment for or recovering from various forms of cancer. As in all Being Human workshops, we did an exercise where participants are asked to surrender and become aware of and act out their own animal nature. Although lighthearted and at times quite humorous, this simple and brief exercise does in fact give people a taste of the animal qualities they carry. In the case of these cancer patients, their animals were certainly wounded, and profoundly affected by the emotional turmoil of their illnesses.*

> *As the exercise began, we noticed a man who immediately appeared drawn to this particular group of women. We watched his careful approach as he edged closer and closer. Sensing a potential threat, the women quickly moved to what they perceived as "safer ground." Despite the adversities these women were facing in their lives, each of them was able to access an animal force that was bigger than that of the potential "predator." In discovering their own self-reliance, they were able to strike back at the attacker and drive him away. It was a beneficial experience for everyone involved. The man was able to recognize the part of him that was predatory, and it was an inspiring show of animal fortitude that revealed new survival patterns and pathways for each of these women that they were then able to apply in their everyday lives and in their fight to recover.—Alicia*

The animal brain is a very large part of our neural makeup, and it is the aspect of us that enables us to lead, group, protect, move, and remember. The motor and sensory cortex, cerebellum and the more primitive vegetative limbic system are the parts of the human nervous system that allow the animal to function. These mediate and, when necessary override the autonomic function of the organs (such as circulation, respiration, and excretion) so that we can go into overdrive when under stress, or go into rest and recuperation when danger has passed. These components of our mammalian brain create strategies that enable us to defend, protect, scavenge, hunt, and move. Our joints, muscles, and fascia are the components that help us react to stimuli and move through life.

Our instincts provide us with an innate sense of how to survive in a competitive or threatening environment. The key to survival is the ability to be attentive to our surroundings, so that we are prepared to react when necessary. We see this in animals that raise their hackles, prick up their ears in response to a strange sound, or focus on a shadow or inconsistency in their field of vision. There is an awareness that something has entered their space or territory. This animal dynamic enables humans to do the same thing. By being present and attentive to our surroundings we can stay out of trouble, circumvent a problem, be on guard, and be prepared to defend.

> When out walking with our dog Tundra, we often pass a wooded area that sometimes has deer in it. Some days she will trot along, very relaxed. Other times her ears go up, her gait is higher, and her whole body becomes attentive to what might be in the trees. On those days there are usually deer present, and she is able to sense them from a hundred yards away with no visual signals. Her attentiveness reminds me of the times that I have been woken during the night by a sound; suddenly my whole body is alert, attentive, listening for another sound, so I can decide if it is something I need to be concerned about or not.—Alicia

One of the defining characteristics of an animal is its habitual behavior. Animals are the ultimate creatures of habit. They have a remarkable ability to "track"— that is, to follow the same route time and time again. Their highly developed sensory capacities—whether they are visual, auditory, or olfactory—enable them to sense where they have previously been. Because animals are survival-oriented, they will attempt to repeat the behaviors that succeed at keeping them alive.

Humans demonstrate this tracking or habitual behavior in many ways. We may travel the same routes to work every day, follow a specific career track, think about things in the same ways, and maintain habitual patterns of behavior. It is not surprising that we operate from habitual patterns. The mammalian, autonomic, and reptilian areas of the brain—areas in which erudition and fore-thought do not enter into the picture—program our habitual and instinctual behavior. Our instincts are well honed, and therefore we operate much of our lives in survival or defensive modes.

We may like the idea of breaking out of our habitual routines, going in a new direction, or trying something different. But when something falls too far out-side our comfort zone, it often seems difficult, if not impossible, to accomplish. Sometimes, simply a fear of the unknown can prevent us from taking action. Instead, we tend to slide back into the security of our familiar lifestyles, where our behavior is often dictated by old patterns and habits that take us down the same pathways time and time again.

Most of us will recognize a habitual part of ourselves. Habits can be very use-ful for learning and for maintaining health, order and function. They make life predictable, so that we know what to expect and feel comfortable and secure. Sometimes, however, habitual behavior becomes such a big part of our lives that we feel bored, burned out, depleted, or depressed. When everything is so familiar and orderly that the anticipated outcome is always the same, our senses become dulled. In the absence of any new challenges we lose our flexibility and our ability to widen and do something different. Over time, we may become so used to doing things in one particular way that we lose sight of any alternatives. We may miss opportunities for something different because we do not "look up" from our heavily trodden path. It is our reflective capacity that provides us with the means to differentiate between habitual ways of thinking and acting that can be limiting and those that are beneficial. If we are able to step back and see what we are doing from a new perspective, we can make changes that support us in expanding our options.

In times of uncertainty, when our sense of well-being and comfort is chal-lenged, our tendency is to fall back into the known and familiar rather than venture into uncharted territory. Moving into unfamiliar territory is not characteristic of most animals unless they are pushed to do so out of some survival-based need. Most of us mirror this same preference for remaining

on our home turf, as venturing forth into the unknown often elicits feelings
of fear because we don't know what to expect.

> *On a recent trip to India, my daughter and I spent a few days in a
> small town in the desert state of Rajasthan. On our first evening
> there we decided to walk from our hotel on the outskirts of the city
> into the center of the town. It was a sensory feast, and we ambled
> through the twisted maze of streets and enjoyed the marvelous sights,
> sounds, and smells. Around midnight, we decided to return to our
> hotel, but soon realized that our evening adventure had left us with
> no sense of how to get there. We asked a group of young men who
> were standing alongside the road, and they nodded assuredly that,
> although it was pitch black and nearly deserted, the road we were on
> would take us where we wanted to go.*
>
> *As we walked along, I became very aware of my heightened sense of
> alarm. I had no idea where we were, and no means to clearly com-
> municate with most of the local people. I grew increasingly protective
> of my teenage daughter, feeling responsible for her safety as well. Only
> then did I realize that my fear was actually occluding my ability to know
> which way to go and what to do next. Once I recognized this, I sought
> the help of a man who, despite the lateness of the hour, was grooming
> his camel on the side of the road. As I described where we were staying,
> he smiled and pointed in the opposite direction. Although I was still a
> little unnerved, I did have the feeling that he was genuinely trying to
> assist us. He hitched up his camel and we climbed aboard his cart, ar-
> riving at our hotel a few minutes later without incident.*—Alexandra

Most of us feel fearful because, when we encounter a situation for which
our limbic system has no previously recorded experience, the system will
interpret it as a previous incident that we experienced as threatening, difficult, dangerous, or risky. This is usually because, in some way, we have
moved beyond our familiar "territory." Fear is a survival response that
prompts an animal to be on guard because the outcome of a situation is unknown. Sometimes we are afraid of things because archetypes or genetic
memories of which we are not even aware govern how we feel.

One night I suddenly awoke, gripped by an awful feeling of fear. I felt sick, my body shook and I was overcome by a feeling of dread that something had happened to our son Lachlan. He had left with two friends to climb to the snowcapped peak of Mount Hood by moonlight and snowboard down in the morning. I started to think that maybe my feeling was a premonition; that he would die. My mind conjured up all sorts of gruesome scenarios. The force of this fear completely took power over me, and my concerns seemed absolutely real. This sudden anxiety was very out of character, as I am used to my children's adventures and don't usually worry about them.

My disquiet woke Solihin. We talked about what was happening with me and then decided to surrender together; I knew that really all I could do was surrender and trust that Lachlan was fine. Gradually, I began to feel quieter. We asked to be shown what I needed to understand, and I saw that I had allowed the force of this feeling of fear to take power and become completely dominant.

My experience in the middle of the night was a potent reminder of the action of the forces, and in particular of how I allow my feelings to take power. When this happens, they paralyze me and prevent me from seeing what is real and what is not. When I surrendered again, I came back to a place of stillness, as if the forces within me had settled into to their rightful order. I soon felt quiet, and we finally fell asleep. I awoke in the morning feeling fine, with no residue of fear or concern, and when a smiling Lachlan walked through the door later that day, the whole experience seemed rather surreal.

On reflection, I realized that the fear that gripped me that night was not related to Lachlan as much as it was to me. I recognized that it may have been more about what Lachlan's climb represented to me: that in life it is "risky" to attempt to climb to the top, to truly put myself "out there" and speak my truth.—Alicia

As humans, we can choose whether or not to let our fear dictate our actions. Those of us dominated by the force of our fear will probably have great diffi-culty moving beyond our established boundaries—whether they are physical, emotional, or mental. Moreover, if these fears become too large, they can lead

Being Human

Family birth order represents a hierarchy that can dictate how we interact in other groups and in society at large.

If our animal nature is carnivorous, one or two big meals a day will usually satisfy our needs. Conversely, those of us who graze all day are more like herbivores. Others might be omnivores, a mixture of the two, which means that their eating habits will be more varied.

to phobias or other irrational thoughts, so that we begin to see everything as a potential danger or threat, which will put us into a protective or defensive reactive state. Being fearful can make us overprotective of our children, which may prevent them from learning to take care of themselves (developing their own animal nature), or from developing their sense of curiosity and discovery. This in turn diminishes their capacity to be attentive to and prepared for danger when it actually is present—the opposite of our intended result!

When we spend most of our time in a highly structured, confined, or sedentary environment, we restrict the range of our animal's movement and activity. One of the most vital aspects of an animal is its ability to play, which provides social interaction, exercise, and, of course, fun. When inactive over long periods of time, our animal may "hibernate" by becoming slow and limited by familiar pathways and habitual behaviors. This lack of physical activity can impair our physiology by limiting the energy available for movement and action.

Animals are instinctively territorial. The notion of territoriality is quite evident in most of our lives. At home, we tend to claim certain areas as "ours," staking out our favorite room, place on the couch, or perhaps even a particular chair at the dinner table. Bedrooms are also a good example of personal territory. We usually make them off-limits to guests, and prefer that those entering knock to announce their arrival into our domain. In our workshops we have noticed how people tend to sit in the same place each day, and after a while others leave that space for them, as it is recognized as "theirs." As workshop facilitators we sometimes intentionally sit in someone else's place, or suggest that everyone sit in a different spot, in order to bring this dynamic to their attention.

Our friend and colleague Maurice was a teacher in an elementary school in central London. His class was composed of immigrants from many different countries, which created a fairly tumultuous atmosphere. After learning about the life forces, Maurice decided to put his new understanding into practice. He asked all the children what kind of animal they thought they might be, and their responses indicated that some were carnivores, others were omnivores, and some were herbivores. He then rearranged the class according to the different types of animals–predators such as lions and wolves on one side, and deer and other animals that could be prey on the other. The change was immediate and remarkable: the previously chaotic environment was transformed into a peaceable kingdom.—Alicia

How we interact with or position ourselves within a group correlates to our instinctive sense of our rank or place within that group. This is often based on our familial environments and past experiences. We may jockey for position, speak up and assume a prominent role, retreat to the periphery and observe, or simply blend into the rest of the group.

The human equivalent of an animal "herd" is a group of people who feel or act in a particular way or who hold similar beliefs or convictions. When many people have the same belief, it creates a strong force. The larger the group, the stronger the force of their belief, whether positive or negative, becomes. This collective force is sometimes so strong that we just get swept along, and our personal beliefs are overridden. This animal dynamic forms a collective consciousness, which is evident in any group of like-minded individuals such as a political party, group of activists, sports team, religious group, club, or fraternity. On a larger scale, a country demonstrates a collective consciousness when the majority unites behind a particular cause. Sharing strong beliefs can be unifying and can place order and structure into society. Sometimes, however, the force of a collective consciousness can turn destructive, as in the mob mentality that incites riots and racial violence.

Wearing the colors, uniform, or insignia of a particular group identifies its members, making them recognizable to themselves and others. This fosters a sense of belonging to the "tribe."

Just as in the animal kingdom, members of a group who are seen as a threat or as "different" from the collective may be attacked or ostracized. This also happens on an individual basis when we automatically label anyone who does not look, act, or think like us as "not of our herd." Doing this as humans may preserve the sanctity of our small circle of life, but it eliminates the opportunity to widen beyond the imaginary, self-imposed boundaries that separate us from other members of the human race.

Do you not know, O people, that I have made you into tribes and nations that you may know each other.
—The Qur'an

| 89 |

Several years ago, I traveled to Seattle on a business trip. One evening after work, my colleague and I walked down the street to a lovely outdoor café. The streets were bustling with people who, like us, were out to enjoy the beautiful weather. As we sipped our drinks, I happened to notice an enormously tall man approaching. He was some distance away, but he appeared to be staring directly at me. "Nonsense!" I told myself, passing my feeling off to my overactive imagination.

As the man passed by our table, however, he stopped and leaned down, as if preparing to say something to me. I glanced at my male companion, who, sensing my fear, simply leaned forward and stared intensely at the man. Suddenly, the man stood upright, exclaimed, "Oh, wow!" and hurried off down the sidewalk. Even in the absence of uttering any words, my friend had communicated in no uncertain terms that the man should move along.

Sometimes the animal part of us won't let go of ideas, feelings, behaviors, or some collective consciousness. We are then like a dog that sinks its teeth into something and won't let go.

Now, more than seven years later, I understand in a very different way what happened that evening. In those days, I had no practical understanding of the life forces, much less a recognition of the animal part of me that was capable of defending myself when necessary. Moreover, I viewed anyone who was "different" from me as a threat and immediately reacted out of my fear. Certainly there are bona fide situations in which we need to be wary; but at that time, I had no ability to determine when that reaction was appropriate. Simply adhering to the known and familiar is one way to get through life, but it undoubtedly limits the possibility of experiencing something new.—Alexandra

We need to maintain the health and strength of the animal self by nourishing, exercising, and resting it, so that, when faced with potential challenges, whether physical or emotional, it is able to perform effectively. Genetics, environment, feelings, and dietary intake all play a critical role in the development of a vigorous animal. Although proper nourishment of the animal is paramount, what constitutes "proper" is unique for each of us. Rather than assuming that one way of eating works for everyone, we should be attentive to what our own animal needs to eat. This will vary depending on the circumstances. There may be times when we need to include meat in our diet, and times when we are better suited to vegetarian foods. If we adopt a diet that is incompatible with our physiology, we may find ourselves unable to support a robust and dynamic animal. In addition, when we inappropriately feed our animal with alcohol, drugs, or even junk food, we impair its ability to serve our needs and react swiftly to defend and protect us.

While teaching in Austria in 1993, I was traveling late at night on the tram in Vienna. I had enjoyed dinner and wine with friends, and although I had

not been drinking heavily, my natural agility and alertness were a little impaired. As I exited the tram, I lost my footing on a high curb, stumbling slightly, but recovering quickly enough to continue moving. At that moment, I was keenly aware that my gait was off and I was somewhat out of step. Suddenly, I noticed something out of the corner of my eye; a man who had casually been loitering near the tram stop abruptly changed his stance and gazed directly at me. Instinctively, I knew that trouble was lurking nearby.

I began to walk toward my destination. I crossed the main street, but instead of walking along the main thoroughfare, I made a sudden and sharp turn down a side road. As I did so, I glanced back and noticed that this stranger had followed ten or so yards behind. As I neared my apartment building I stopped, pretending to take an interest in something in a shop window, but actually to gauge the man's behavior. The man stopped as well, still some yards behind me. With my heart pounding, I walked to the entrance door, grasped my key, quickly turned the lock, and went inside. Silently, I watched in the darkness and safety of the hallway as the man's shadow passed in front of the door. A moment later he passed by once again, and I saw the doorknob slowly begin to turn. Fortunately, the door was locked, and his attempt to enter failed. I continued to watch the shadowy figure as it then moved away from my door and off into the night.

This scenario is a perfect demonstration of the predator and the prey. Human creatures that prey on others look for animal weaknesses. They observe the movement of the body, and they sense an easy mark, such as one who is under the influence of drugs or alcohol, or one who appears lost or afraid. I am certain that this man was alerted by his basic animal instincts to my state of impairment, and knew that I might not be fully on guard.—Solihin

The necessity of having a strong animal is reflected in many self-defense classes, in which participants are encouraged to practice walking tall and looking confident and attentive. It is widely recognized that the predator spots those who appear weak, unsure, lost, or unprotected as potential victims. Rarely would a predator make a random attack on someone who appears strong and able to protect themselves, as there is too much risk of failure.

Our animal defense mechanisms are represented in our physiology by our skin, mucous membranes, digestive juices and acids, and immune system. When functioning properly, these components of our "first line of defense" have the capacity to differentiate what is alien from what is self, and to attack that which is foreign. The various components of the immune system act as barriers that protect us from foreign invasion. Their job is not only to destroy that which penetrates these barriers, but also to identify and destroy mutations that have originated within the body, such as cancer cells. When different people are exposed to a virus or other pathogen, only those with a strong immune system will be able to defend themselves against invasion. Conversely, those with a compromised animal are much more susceptible to penetration, and therefore to illness. Our culture encourages us to rely on the myriad pills, potions, and other external remedies to rid ourselves of symptoms, rather than prompting us to reflect on the ontology of the problem—the factors that have predisposed us to develop our current dysfunction.

The similarity between animals and humans does not end with our defensive and protective mechanisms. Our hormonal system parallels that of the animal kingdom by regulating our growth and sleep cycles and by enabling us to react and adapt to new environments, formulate strategies, and initiate and send neurological signals. It also plays a vital role in human sexuality by governing our cyclical rhythms and proclivity for sexual interaction. It is our animal self that physically engages in sexual activity.

Within the animal kingdom, sex is driven by instincts that are governed by pheromones, chemicals secreted to attract a prospective mate. Male and female animals are therefore "programmed" to foster the survival of the species. The male is driven to inseminate, the female to receive the seed. In a herd, the males will compete for the top position to ensure that only the biggest and strongest animals impregnate the females in order to proliferate the species.

In human society, sexual roles are much more complex, because our sexuality is influenced by all of the life forces. With so many factors affecting it, it is both viewed and expressed in many different ways. As a sacred act of intimacy, sex epitomizes the ideals of union and love. Some sexual acts are, however, motivated simply by the drive to dominate or exert power over someone.

For most of us, our sexual relationships fall somewhere between these two extremes, and can vary according to our state, our partner, and the situation.

As the feeling of our sexuality develops, we use our animal instincts to find a suitable partner. The selection of a prospective mate is an interesting human phenomenon. A study by researchers at the University of Chicago offers solid evidence that humans both produce and react to pheromones. These chemicals contain a scent that is hormonal (animal) in origin, and they signal a prospective partner's sexual state and readiness. We process these signals, even if unconsciously, along with many other pieces of interpretive data such as our personal history, genetic predisposition, feelings, physical attraction, and intellectual appeal, all of which add to the complexity of choosing a partner.

Our sexual behavior emerges from what is seeded within our genetic coding and from our environment (our memories and experiences). We each contain the inherited patterns of our parents' sexuality. In addition, growing up in a warm and affectionate family supports us in developing our own intimate relationships. If our environment did not provide any real love or affection, however, or if our parents' relationship caused feelings of distrust or pain, we might reject (an animal response) these familial patterns. But because we contain some 50 percent of each of our parent's DNA, their underlying dynamic will still be present within our genetic coding. The behavioral patterns we inherit, in the form of our genetic makeup, do influence our behavior, including our sexual behavior—even if in the most subtle of ways. Obviously the nuances are our own, but the predispositions—both positive and negative—are built into us.

Unlike animals, humans have sex for a myriad of reasons, all of which reflect our state at any given time. Our feelings are an integral part of our intimate interactions. We may wish to express the depth of our love for our partner, or find a way to feel connected to ourself or to another. We may feel playful, or seek ways to have new experiences. We may use sex to explore, or to feel alive and desirable. Perhaps we seek to nourish our feelings, or to attain a sense of power. If we feel empty, we may want a partner who can fill the void. If we are sad, we may find solace in the arms of another. If we are angry, we may sublimate our feelings through hard or rough sex. The force of our feelings will affect those of our partner, because during intercourse the force of the man penetrates the woman, and the force of the woman envelops the man. Both of these forces can remain with the individuals even after intercourse. It is therefore important that we are aware of our state and the force that motivates us to engage in sex, and the effect that our feelings might have on ourself and our partner.

If we mask our true scent with perfumes and deodorants, a prospective mate may not be able to sense whether we are a compatible partner.

Some people have an animal that has been wounded, whether physically, emotionally, or psychologically. Sometimes our physical scars actually hold the residue of pain, feelings, or experience. These wounds, and their resultant memories, often linger long after any physical damage has been repaired. As we move forward in life, the pain of unresolved wounds resurfaces and our resulting behavior reflects this wounded state. This is what happens when we overreact to something with words or actions, erupt in anger, or retreat in tears and isolation. Our animal is, metaphorically speaking, licking its wounds.

We often choose partners who in some way resonate with our own genetic coding.

In our workshops we encourage participants to recognize the impaired or wounded state of their animal nature, if they feel that is what they are carrying. Then we remind them that, through prayer and surrender to God, we open the possibility for those wounds to be cleaned and begin to heal. Most important, we ask each of them to simply to make the space for their healthy animal self to emerge. Even if we initially must imitate this behavior, the healthy animal will eventually begin to manifest within us.

As teens, most of us are interested in sex because the neo-cortex is not fully developed until adulthood. Consequently, our mammalian (animal) brain is the dominant working machinery.

When we are able to observe and reflect on our actions, play, habits, and sexuality, the role of our animal self becomes clear. Our animal instinctively plays out the dynamics of hierarchy in the external world as we try to find our "place" in a family, relationship, job, or society. This also occurs inside us as the material, vegetative, animal, and human forces jostle for position. When one of these takes power it disturbs the natural order of the hierarchy. In this way, we may find that our emotions and feelings, genetic predispositions, or animal proclivities have become the proverbial "master of the house." When the human house is out of order we might feel stuck, ill, lost, depressed, disorganized, or unsupported. Our life forces must stay in their correct order to serve and support the human.

The evolution of the human neocortex and the prefrontal lobes of the brain enables us to transcend our basic animal instincts. Our humanity is shaped by these neurological centers of higher reasoning and reflective thought. This allows us to choose how to utilize our various animal penchants. As humans, the animal gives us the courage to forge new pathways of behavior, remain in step with life, and squarely face that which we need to see—our shadows, feelings, and relationships—so that we know what we need to do and can take action. When we know, value, and master our own animal nature, it can and will serve, defend, protect, and support us.

Being Human

11

Reflectiveness

busy mind
mental confusion
scattered thoughts
on stepping back
surrendered
the vision comes
suddenly, unexpected

Each of us contains the capacity to rise above our animal nature and see things from a different perspective. This third essential human quality is reflectiveness, which bridges our animal and human selves, and is represented by a pair of wings. We can compare our human reflective capacity to that of an eagle, which has the ability to soar high above the ground in order to change perspective, gaining clarity and farsightedness. It is this quality that allows us to respond to stimuli as humans, rather than react as animals do.

Many years ago, on holiday in Greece, Alicia and our friend Maurice were swimming in the warm Aegean Sea. Maurice wore a hat to shade his bald pate, his beard trailed in the water, and his pink face contrasted against the white shirt he wore to protect his fair English skin against the burning sun. He was a schoolteacher whose home displayed his love of reading and knowledge. It was full of books, which were piled high on every shelf and in every corner; at times, his erudition put him at loggerheads with others.

Maurice and Alicia swam out to a small wooden platform some seventy yards from the shore to relax in the sun. As they talked, he asked about the nature of our work. Alicia explained the idea of the forces and their relationship to the caduceus. As the afternoon waned, they swam back to shore, and Maurice set off to the village overlooking the bay.

Later that evening, a very excited Maurice came into the café where we were eating to relay an extraordinary experience. He spoke of climbing the dusty, cobbled street up to the small village on the hill-side, where he had hoped to find solace in a shaded taverna from the unrelenting sun. As he walked into the square of the village, something above him caught his eye. He looked up and saw an eagle clutching in its talons a wriggling snake. As he watched, fascinated, his earlier conversation with Alicia came flooding back, for two of the

components of the caduceus were above him. Other people passed by, appearing unaffected by, unaware of, or perhaps not interested in the eagle and the struggling snake circling above them.

Maurice felt that he had been given a gift concerning his own nature. He suddenly understood that over the years he had adopted a pattern that enabled his active and erudite mind to take him off into high-flying thoughts. His constant reflectiveness kept him isolated, separate, and cerebral. This intellectual loftiness removed him from his emotions and feelings. Like the eagle who swoops down to kill the snake, his mind would kill off his capacity to access and widen his feelings.—Solihin

Reflectiveness gives us the unique ability to consider and ruminate upon a vast range of information. We then have the opportunity to get off the beaten track by rising up out of old familiar patterns, feelings, behaviors, and thoughts into the realm of greater possibilities. Our reflective capacity enables us not only to "see" what is occurring, but moreover, to take action to change by offering us new solutions to old problems.

Reflectiveness allows us to move from the instinctive animal self to the creative human self. It enables us to see all the different facets of a person or situation.

In order to be truly reflective, both integrity and flexibility need to be present. It is the motivating force of integrity that prompts us to rise up out of the old and also "grounds" our otherwise lofty thoughts. When accompanied by flexibility, this gives us a width of consciousness that allows us to see things from a new—and often very different—perspective.

When our second daughter, Rebecca, was very young, she had nightmares that woke her. After many broken nights I decided to work with her to help us both understand why this was happening. During this process we discovered that her integrity was in its infancy. Metaphorically, she had no tree or staff upon which her eagle could roost at night, making her mind "fly high" with very active dreams that would cause her to cry out and wrestle her way out of sleep mode. Even at an early age, Rebecca was by nature very insightful, asking questions and illustrating a depth of thought that belied her years. Because she needed to develop her connection with her inner self and with the Divine, however, her active mind did not rest at night.

What were we to do with someone at such a tender age? I felt that she needed to connect with and be comforted by her angel. At the time my own understanding of angels was limited, although I felt that we each have one that looks after us. While tucking her up in bed that night, I asked her if she knew that she had an angel. She replied yes, but she also said she didn't really know whether angels were real. I asked her to call her angel to her, and to feel what happened when it came. She became quiet and surrendered, just as we had practiced over the years at meal times and as prayer. I felt a definite change in the room, and then Rebecca opened her eyes to tell me that she had felt a tingle all over her body. I said this was her way to know that her angel was there. She settled down and fell asleep, a smile of contentment on her face.

Each night from then on, Rebecca would surrender and ask her angel to come. She felt connected and protected as she experienced her angel's presence. This was the beginning of the development of her fledgling integrity—her connection to the Divine and to her own inner self. From that first night her nightmares ceased.—Solihin

In the absence of integrity our thoughts may become ungrounded, lofty, and out of touch with reality. This is what happens when our reflective capacity (the eagle) flies away, but doesn't come home to roost. Conversely, there are times when we are so anchored to the old that we are unable to rise up and take flight.

Many years ago, while walking in a park in England, I came across a man carrying a hawk on his leather-gauntleted wrist. I stopped to admire the bird and we began to talk about hawks and eagles. I mentioned seeing a film of a bald eagle catching fish, and how amazed I was by the eagle's capacity to swoop down to the water and emerge with a large fish in its talons. "Ah," he said, "but did you know that if the fish is too big or heavy, the eagle is unable to let go?" He explained that the eagle's claws contain a locking mechanism that prevents it from losing its hold. Without the ability to release its talons, an eagle cannot rise out of the water if it has seized a fish that is too heavy, often resulting in its own drowning. Sometimes fishermen even catch salmon with the talons of an eagle embedded in their bodies.—Alicia

We, too, sometimes have a tendency to latch onto something that ultimately drags us down. Our inability to let go can prevent us from rising up into true reflectiveness, as we "drown" in old habits, feelings, patterns, beliefs, and ways of thinking that do not enable us to see things from a different and wider perspective. Just as the eagle has to land to be able to release its grip, we, too, need to be able to ground ourselves (find our integrity) in order to be able to let go of something that is no longer needed.

Sometimes we manifest the qualities of a vulture in our thinking; we metaphorically keep picking away at something that is already "dead" (perhaps an old feeling or grievance, or some past event or trauma). We find that we cannot leave it alone, and keep returning for a few more pecks. Eating old, dead food time and time again may be fine for a vulture, whose digestion can handle decaying matter, but it is generally not good for us to be nourished or fed off old traumas, old scenarios, and old "what ifs." This is very much like picking at a scab that never has a chance to heal because of the constant attention it receives.

There is a mythological creature known as the Harpy, which is a greedy, winged, half-woman, half-bird monster with sharp claws. Many of us will recognize—in ourselves and in others—a tendency to continually "harp" on some idea, thought, or emotion with little respite. When our minds are thus engaged and preoccupied there is no mental quietness—no true reflection—so we cannot hear or listen to our inner selves.

Sometimes when we see things differently from others it can be uncomfortable because it may put us outside the "herd."

The first step in changing these behaviors that limit our reflective capacity is to notice that they exist. Then, through surrender, we can ask for help in releasing our obsessive tendencies or the dead weight of those ideas, feelings, or behaviors that drag us down. To accept that something happened and be willing to let it go enables us to move forward in our lives.

> *Shortly after Peter and I married, my in-laws inaugurated a new tradition in the form of an annual family reunion to Charleston, South Carolina. Although the beach is lovely and the area is rich with southern charm and tradition, after the first few years I voiced a strong objection to going to the same location every single summer. Growing up, my family's vacations were quite varied, and they included trips back east, out west, a hotel at the beach one year, camping in the mountains the next, and so forth. I*

wanted our children to sample a wide variety of Americana in their youth, as I had been able to do. I battled Peter every year when "the week" was upon us, resolutely sticking to my guns that it was unreasonable for us to commit to vacationing in what I saw as "the same old place with the same people." One year I even agreed to go, but affirmed that our family would not eat meals with the rest of the clan, but would dine on our own.

Then in 1993 my father passed away after a brief but intense bout with cancer. I spent many months wishing that I had had more time to know who he was, to learn more about his life and how he saw the world. I longed to ask him questions that would forever remain unanswered, to engage in the deep conversations that would now never take place.

Gradually my perspective on the family reunion began to change. I started to look forward to the week and the opportunity to sit and chat with members of my extended family, to ponder the events of the world, our kids, our lives, or even just who-would-make-what for dinner that night. It is a time of connection that I now cherish greatly, despite the fact that nothing in the scenario has changed—nothing, that is, except my viewpoint.—Alexandra

In classical Greek mythology, wings are used to convey an important message about reflectiveness. Winged sandals, helmets, and steeds serve as reminders of the perils of unbridled reflective thought and imagination that can take people into ungrounded realms, illusions, or the depths of their shadows. These mythic stories enable us to see when our reflective capacity may be constrained by the force of our material, vegetative, animal, or human natures.

Hermes, the god of the underworld, wore winged sandals on his feet. When our thoughts fly into the darkness of our own personal shadows—our gloom and doom mentality—we wear the wings of our reflectiveness on our feet and are reflecting on the world through our material nature. This type of reflectiveness is useful when we need to observe what we hide in the dark recesses of our minds, but isn't helpful if we continually wear these shoes.

Likewise, we might place our reflective wings onto our emotions and view the world through our feelings. Like Peter Pan, we fly into Never Never Land and never

grow up (out of our emotions), and thus stay in a world colored by feelings that are seductive, yet illusory. Similarly, some of us flit about like Tinkerbell, moving from feeling to feeling as our winged emotions change from moment to moment.

When we fly over familiar terrain and always go into the known, we become like Pegasus, the winged horse. This means our reflectiveness is then limited by our habitual and instinctive thinking and does not represent a width of consciousness.

Mercury wore wings on his helmet and was seen as the communicator to the gods. This winged thought allows us to soar unfettered into the realms of the muse to bring back imagery and ideas less earthbound. Icarus, however, fell to his death when his waxed (manmade) wings melted because he flew too close to the heat of the sun—a reminder that manmade thoughts that become too lofty may ultimately bring us crashing back to earth.

Although there are some people who have an innate reflective ability, most of us cultivate this quality during our lifetime. Initially, it is our home environment that supports its development. If we observe our parents reflecting on their own lives and the world around them and are encouraged to question and explore, the seeds of reflectiveness are sown. In addition, many of us have the opportunity to develop our reflective thought through education. Schools that require vigorous essay writing and encourage debate among students prompt them to step back and gain a wider perspective on what is going on around them. Rote learning, on the other hand, does not foster reflective thought, and it may be a moot point whether multiple-choice exams elicit any real reflection or simply the mere processing of fact—the accumulation and storage of data for later retrieval.

At a physical level, reflective thought requires the functioning of many of our neural components, in particular our mammalian brain and temporal lobes. Through these we can not only gather and reference all our experiences, emotions, habitual patterns, and defensive ways of thinking, but also rise above them to see other possibilities. This is the origin of creativity, where seed ideas deep within us are given new possibilities to grow.

Our capacity to be reflective arises from the unique neural architecture of the human brain. The wings on the symbol of the caduceus mirror the wing-shaped ventricles of the brain. These spaces within each cerebral hemisphere expand as they fill with cerebral spinal fluid, and partially empty as they contract. The walls of the ventricles are made up of nuclei that are part of our limbic system. Cranial osteopathy recognizes that in a healthy person the brain and its fluid moves in a particular and predictable rhythm every six seconds, which is echoed throughout the entire body. When our thoughts, beliefs, philosophies, habits and emotional states influence us, their force interferes with this innate rhythmical movement, which affects and alters the mechanics and function of our physiology. In Solihin's clinical experience as a cranial osteopath he has observed that when people are suffering from various dysfunctions—psychoses, habitual patterns, depression, or other emotional states—they demonstrate many peculiarities within the structure of the brain and its movement.

Spending too much of our time in our thinking is like only inhabiting one small corner of our house.

The practice of Kundalini yoga alters perception through exercises that manipulate the spine, reversing the normal flow of cerebral spinal fluid, and sending back a wave of fluid into the ventricles, causing them to expand beyond normal limits. When this happens, it may cause an intense emotional release, and a sense of transcendence and bliss.

Those known for their prodigious minds often had their momentous "ahas" via a dream as with Einstein, or during a moment of relaxation as with Archimedes in his bath.

It is interesting to note that some patients who have had electric shock treatment have ventricles that appear to be in "full flight" position—expanded beyond their normal limits by the force of the electricity. As a result, the patient becomes less held to their emotional vicissitudes (the memories stored in the limbic system), which moves them—either permanently or temporarily—out of chronic depression and forms of psychosis.

Expansion of the ventricles causes the temporal lobes to both rotate and expand. Some modern research is now linking temporal lobe activity to transcendence, spiritual experience, and out-of-body states. There are those who suggest that the temporal lobes are the source of our godly experiences and visionary moments. Others maintain that they are merely a physiological reference point from which we interpret those experiences that come from the Divine.

When we are held in the strictures of habitual thought and old emotions, the temporal lobes of the brain are inhibited—the ventricles are not able to fully expand. This inhibition appears to prevent us from having a wider sense of ourself and our purpose and a greater worldview. Expansion of these temporal lobes occurs as we develop, adopt, and utilize a reflective capacity that takes us into the realm of new possibilities and creative thought. We need to be able to move beyond the force of our cultural, emotional, and habitual viewpoints.

When life is routine and habitual, we may not exercise much reflection. We go through the motions, do what we have to do, and come home to rest and get ready for the next day. Most of us turn on the television or computer, or bury ourselves in a book, entertaining our minds so that our thoughts are directed by what we see, hear, or read. If we spend a large part of our time watching television or surfing the Web, we may adopt the rhythm or pace of the visual world and inhabit it for long periods of the day. This exposure to huge amounts of information, constantly moving images, and changes of scene and tempo shape how we see the world. If this becomes our visual reference point, we may develop minds that are better equipped to take in and record information than they are to reflect upon it. All forms of communication provide seed ideas for personal reflection. The question is, do we allow the various forms of input to have power over us, or do we use them as a resource?

The willingness to question is an integral part of reflectiveness. Do we routinely accept as truth all that we are told, all that we read, hear on the radio, or see on television, or are we willing to consider other viewpoints, as challenging as that might be? Do we recognize how fear can lead us to clamp down into reaction, rather than expanding to see the big picture? Are we willing to look at ourselves, face our own limitations, question our own beliefs of who we are and how we fit it to the scheme of things, and consider the deeper possibilities for our own lives?

> *We have a beautiful book called "The Home Planet," which contains photos of the earth from space with comments from those who have seen it from that perspective. One astronaut who was part of an international team described how, when they first saw the earth, each astronaut pointed out his own country. As time passed, each man pointed out his continent. By the fifth day, they were aware of only one earth, home to all of them. How different our world might be if our leaders could see the earth, our communal home, from such a broad perspective!*—Alicia

There are those who believe that we create our own reality by the power of our thoughts. Many of us would agree, because we recognize how deeply the force of our thoughts and feelings influences and affects our lives. If we have a pessimistic view of life, we may find ourselves faced with obstacles, illnesses, and difficulties. Conversely, a positive outlook and attitude can open up possibilities and enable us to see things we might otherwise miss. As extraordinary and significant as the mind is, it does have its limitations. If we believe the mind holds the answers to all the great questions or is the conduit to all of life, we may be very disappointed to discover that it, too, is simply made of material, which will one day again become dust. When our mind dies or becomes defunct through an illness such as Alzheimer's disease, then what we thought was a "spiritual" organ suddenly becomes powerless. By being present, attentive, and reflective, our inner selves can begin to develop so that we are not totally dependent on our minds to provide the answers or direction in our lives.

The human mind needs to be educated, but it also needs to be illuminated. By surrendering to the Great Life, the power of the mind becomes less dominant and our learning and thoughts can be illuminated. When the mind is quiet, the opportunity to receive something new arises. This metaphorical warming of the fertile grounds of our imagination (creative thinking) may bring to life something unexpected.

Many years ago, towards the end of our first visit to Oregon, Solihin and I sat on the top of a mountain in eastern Oregon, reflecting upon the adventures and experiences we had had during the past two weeks. The trip represented a quest for us, and we wondered where it would lead and what its purpose was. As we pondered those questions, I noticed three eagles circling in front of us, so closely that I could see the colors of their feathers. As I watched them, I suddenly had a vision of Solihin and myself working together and having a place where people could come to receive what they needed in their lives. I was not sure what this meant, as at the time we were living in England and had no plans to work together.

As the months passed, it became clear to us that we should begin to lead workshops together, and various signs started to point towards America. Once our direction was clear, I never doubted what we were

doing. Two-and-a-half years later we arrived in Oregon to begin a new life with our family. The presence of the eagles that day had given us a reminder of the importance of being reflective, and the subsequent vision had enabled us to broaden our horizons enough to do something we had not previously considered.—Alicia

At an inner level, reflectiveness signifies the illumination, by Grace, of that which we have not previously known. It is our prepared mind waiting for the Light. As with everything, there is a duality. Pursuit of knowledge can foster reflection, but true illumination comes only from surrender to God. Through the practice of surrender, our mind gradually becomes our servant. We need to prepare the mind, but also to let God touch it.

12

The Human Self

Not Christian or Jew or Muslim, not Hindu,
Buddhist, Sufi, or Zen. Not any religion or cultural system
I belong to the Beloved, have seen the two worlds as one
and that one call to and know, first, last, outer, inner,
only that breath breathing human being.

—Jelaluddin Rumi

Beginning to recognize and understand your own material, vegetative, and animal forces and how they shape and influence your life is one small but significant part of a much larger picture. Because each of us is a microcosm of the earth and its elements, the forces that we carry are also mirrored in our external world. As we notice and come to value the resources with which we have been provided, we will find a deeper appreciation for the earth, which not only resonates with the collective history of mankind, but also provides the foundation and source of support for all of life. As we come to understand how the vegetative system within us nourishes, cleans, and expands our feeling nature, we will become aware of the intrinsic value of the vegetative systems of the earth, such as the forests and jungles of our world, which do the same for our environment. As we come to know our power, our will, our sexuality and our tribe, we will become attentive of all that the animal world brings to our lives and to the life of our planet.

Just as the human within us is the steward of our material, vegetative, and animal selves, we as humans have a responsibility to steward the earth and its plant and animal life. When we are not congruent within ourselves, we often do not consider our responsibility to the kingdoms that comprise the world around us, but instead deplete and exhaust these resources simply to fulfill our own needs and desires. Through our surrender to the Great Life, our own life forces become ordered and unified and we begin to feel one with all of creation. As this feeling of wholeness develops, we will recognize that we are an essential part of these intricately linked realms that support each other through the interconnectedness of all that exists.

During the writing of this book, Solihin and I went to hear Archbishop Desmond Tutu speak. It was a wonderful and inspiring evening. Among other things, the archbishop spoke of the Zulu word ubuntu. He said, "Ubuntu means my humanity is in your humanity. Someone is only human through other humans. I need other human beings in order to be human. I cannot be human in isolation." Ubuntu expresses a unifying vision of humanity. It regards humanity as an integral part of ecosystems that lead to a communal responsibility to sustain life, where human values are based on social, cultural, and spiritual criteria and the earth's resources are shared on the principle of equity among and between generations.

Ubuntu is the principle of caring for each other's well-being, with respect, empathy, compassion and a spirit of mutual support. Each individual's humanity is ideally expressed through his or her relationship with others. Ubuntu inspires us to open ourselves to others, and to learn of others as we learn of ourselves. This respect for the differences in others is paramount.—Alicia

The human life force acts as a "carrier wave" that contains the full range of races, cultures, beliefs, memories, and aspirations known to mankind. Integrity is the connecting force that enables us to tune into the resonance of all humanity. When truly quiet, we can taste these different qualities at an inner level and appreciate the extraordinary creation and unity behind this expression of life and Divine purpose. This is available to all of us, but most of us are only aware of, and unable to see beyond, our own immediate resonance. The human life force, through our neurology, allows us to think, cognate, reflect, analyze, create, and construct, and to develop language and culture.

We are all human in form, although perhaps not yet all human in content.

The human passion for knowledge compels us to seek an understanding of our world, to know ourselves, and to look beyond the horizon. Perhaps we never question whether we are "human" because we have been endowed with minds that clearly elevate us above the other kingdoms and which have an extraordinary capacity to think, reflect, communicate, imagine, create, dream, and contemplate. What is most important in determining our humanity, however, is not only the presence of our mind, but the way in which we choose to use it. This capacity to make choices gives us an added dimension.

We must continually count on the appearance of new facts, the inclusion of which within the compass of our earlier experience may require a revision of our fundamental concepts.

—Niels Bohr

While it is evident that we make choices all the time, what is less apparent is how often they are influenced by the action of the various forces. The force of our genetic coding, feelings, or instincts often takes power and therefore colors our choices. When the material force dictates, our choices are based on the resonance of the old—our history, forebears, culture, or nation. If the force of our feelings predominates, we might make a choice based on an errant emotion or old hurt. When our animal force is in power, we will choose solely from instinct, habit, the need to survive, or the need to dominate.

When faced with a difficult decision, we always have the choice to seek higher guidance. When we surrender to the Great Life, the mind becomes our servant—open, wide, and receptive. What we experience in our surrender may confirm our choice, or present us with something completely unexpected.

Over time the human self has come to be ruled more and more by thought, instead of by the quietness of the inner feeling or the inner self; so in the end people's hearts and brains are always busy and their inner feeling has almost no opportunity to be at peace.
—Muhammad Subuh

When we are constantly in our heads, our busy brains may exclude—rather than provide us with—useful information from the other parts of ourselves. When we disconnect from our material, vegetative, or animal selves, we allow our minds to take power. Our continual cogitation fuels our capacity to construct false scenarios, which can give rise to a distorted sense of reality. When the integrated human prevails, however, we will recognize the proclivities, nuances, and predominant patterns at every level that influence our choices and motivate our actions.

As a child, I had frequent temper tantrums. My explosive outbursts resulted in a variety of broken objects, including the occasional door or window. Despite the fact that I had three older siblings, nothing had prepared my parents for a child filled with such rage. There seemed to be no rhyme or reason to the resolution of my angry reactions.

As I moved into adulthood, although my destructive outbursts became a thing of the past, the anger that precipitated them did not. Each time I felt that I had been treated unjustly, their memory—regardless of how far removed or unconnected to the present moment these old tantrums were—washed over me, fueling my irritation. Off I would go into some tirade about this or that, never recognizing that I was swinging to an emotional extreme that was much less based on the present than on the collective total of many unresolved past feelings.

Over the last few years, as I have begun to recognize and connect with my integrity and the stillness and quietness within myself, this need to vent my feelings with hurricane force has all but disappeared. I am now able

to see "what's what" in what I feel is a much more balanced way. Do I ever get angry? Of course I do. But I now recognize that there is no need to resort to such wild emotional extremes to make my feelings known. I have made the choice not to let old and often irrelevant emotions govern how I express myself.—Alexandra

We sometimes make errant choices because the brain is very habitual in the way that it structures our thoughts and beliefs. Our beliefs may be embedded in our genetic coding or forged over time through our own experiences, becoming part of our map. Beliefs shape our foundation, feelings, actions, thoughts, identity, and worldview. Some beliefs are so deeply ingrained in us that we become absolutely certain that they are true, despite the fact that there may be evidence to refute them in the world around us. Retaining such beliefs can limit our opportunities to move in new directions. When we recognize the beliefs that we hold, we can then determine whether they are beneficial or detrimental to our lives.

Several years ago we were facilitating a Life Forces workshop in which some people in the group were members of a particular religion whose core belief was that Eve was responsible for mankind's fall from Grace because she had succumbed to the temptation of the serpent. We were talking about flexibility and the snake. The discussion seemed to drag on; it appeared that the topic would never be completed, nor the participants able to experience or really understand it. The force of their belief was so strong that it prevented them from widening their viewpoint.

Realizing we were at an impasse, we asked each of them to hold out an arm and clench their fists as if holding on tightly to something. A few moments later, we asked each of them to notice what was happening to their bodies. Most became aware of the rigidity of their arm and upper body. They realized that when they held onto things so tightly, it mirrored a constriction, not only of their muscles, but also of their hearts, feelings, actions, and thoughts. We then explained that this is exactly what happens when we hold tightly to our beliefs. We asked them to simply relax their grip so that, without letting go of the belief, they nonetheless became less rigid. We hoped that by doing this they would free up a space for

We can't hang onto the old and reach out to the new at the same time.

a wider understanding. In fact, that is exactly what happened, and we were able to move forward with the workshop.—Solihin

Our beliefs deeply influence and shape our attitudes and feelings towards sexuality. Different cultures have various perspectives towards sexuality, and most adopt moral, ethical, or religious codes to govern the complexity of this human need. Some have developed esoteric models to facilitate more inspired acts of creation or intimacy. The classic Indian treatise *The Kama Sutra*, the Arabian *Perfumed Garden*, and Taoist and Buddhist models of sexual tantra all exemplify this. They all acknowledge our need to elevate the act of sexual union to one that is sacred.

Ideally, in sexual union the corresponding forces of each partner meet one another—material to material, feeling (vegetative) to feeling, animal to animal, human to human. Often, however, there is a mismatch of these forces. For example, when a man's animal force penetrates his partner's vegetative, or feeling, nature, a disharmonious state may be created, as she may feel violated. Conversely, if the force of a woman's feelings envelops a man's animal nature, he may feel seduced, disempowered, or defenseless. Perhaps this mismatch is one of the reasons that there is sometimes the feeling that something is missing. Being intimate with another is a challenge for many of us because it means we have to be willing to completely open to our partner, revealing and sharing the deepest parts of our self, and exposing our vulnerabilities without fear of judgment.

The degree to which we engage with our human essence during lovemaking depends on *how* we make love. We might come together out of a sense of duty, enter with pride, seduce through intent, perform habitually, subdue with conquest, or satisfy with power or technique. Or we may do our best to surrender our proclivities, needs and desires so that we can enter into lovemaking with a higher purpose: the union of the two into one. In this way we are able to truly meet and know the essence of one another. This sacred act allows the entry of the noble life force, which can then envelop the union, and bring us into rhythm with our partner. As we rise above the human mind and make sex a union of selves and purpose with another human being, it becomes part of the worship of Life, and the mutually interdependent male and female forces become one. This is the alchemy of the human life force that allows the true human in us to manifest for those moments.

You cannot shake hands with a closed fist.
—Indira Gandhi

Sometimes a feeling of separation, the seeds of which can be sown from our conception onwards, challenges our intimate relationships. We face many different separations throughout our lives, some of which are rites of passage that are essential for our development: our initial separation from the world of spirit as we enter this earthly life; from our mothers at birth; from the breast when weaned, from our innocence at puberty, and from our original families with marriage. If we embrace the idea that one's soul enters the body at the moment of conception, and that union can occur at many different levels, we can see that the state of the parents at the conception of a child is very important. Because the man acts as the conduit for the penetrating force of the One, his state at the time of conception is paramount. A child conceived during a union of oneness and love will feel that support throughout his or her life. If we conceive, or were conceived, unconsciously or from a union where that oneness was missing, however, the embryo may hold the feeling of separation from the world of spirit. The twists and turns of life may then highlight this feeling. We may experience this in relation to others, God, or even our self and our sense of purpose and identity. During childhood, perhaps we were the kid who got sick all the time, was not picked for the team, was bullied or teased, was irritable or ill-tempered, was seen as an outsider, or was shy and retiring. Any of these situations fosters the internal notion of not being one of the group.

When I was thirty-eight, a small, crusty, red area began to develop on my lower back. Initially I ignored it, but over time I recognized that it was a patch of psoriasis, just like the ones my mother had on her hand and sole of her foot. Some years later, I asked her about this apparently inherited pattern. She told me that one of her uncles, a fiery, temperamental, and rather angry man, had also had severe psoriasis. To my surprise, it had developed in both of them at the age of thirty-eight.

This caused me to wonder what human trigger, environmental cause, internal state, or chance occurrence had switched on this pattern of psoriasis. What was the underlying itch? As a consequence, my efforts over the years have been focused on discovering and teaching others an understanding of allergies—psoriasis is an autoimmune allergic mechanism—in the context of the life forces. During this time I have observed this pattern of separation in patients of all ages, including children, who have eczemas, cradle cap, fungus, asthma, colic—even those who are introverted or ill at ease, or generally whom we might term "irritable."

The root of the word psoriasis is **psora**—*from the Hebrew tsorat, meaning "unclean," or "stigma."*

I now understand that when I feel separate or turned away from others, myself, or my connection to God, my psoriasis begins to itch and react. My loss of connection to myself appears to be the force that switches on this particular genome. As soon as I notice this, I surrender and get a sense of what makes me feel separate. It may be that I have forgotten to do my prayers, or that I'm not really present with Alicia or my children. Perhaps I have not phoned my father in England for a while, or I don't feel heard or understood, or I am not listening to my own needs for more rest or play. I then act upon this understanding. I might simply apologize for something that I have said or done, reconnect with someone, or respond to my need. Almost immediately, the itch subsides. In this way I connect to myself and again face life, and see that I am not separate. This has been an undeniable gift.—Solihin

The "gift" of a feeling of separation is that it serves as the impetus for us to find the source of our irritation. Through surrender we can ask to be illuminated about what precipitates our feeling and what to do about it. Perhaps we need to modify a lifestyle that keeps us separate, move beyond a familial pattern that makes us feel outcast, or reclaim our sense of value as a viable member of a group or a partner in a relationship. Most of those who have in some way contributed to our feeling of separation will not understand the consequence of their behavior because they do not recognize the action of the life forces. Remembering the words, "Father, forgive them, for they know not what they do" opens the way for a compassionate heart through which we can clean any old feelings of hurt, abandonment, and separation that we have carried within.

Language is a defining characteristic of humans. The thousands of languages on the earth create human society, prompt intimacy, aid the communication and transmission of knowledge and culture, and allow us to express ourselves in myriad ways. Despite our sophisticated language system, however, we still sometimes manage to have misconceptions, or misinterpret and misunderstand one another. This is when the force of our language can cause division, separation, reaction, or dissent. How does this happen?

It is incumbent upon each of us to be mindful of the part of us that "speaks" when we use language. Do we speak as a human with a wide and open heart? We are certainly all capable of doing that, but we also need to be aware that although our language is uniquely human, our minds do not always function from that part of ourselves. For example, if we feel we are being attacked, we may speak from our protective or instinctive self. Our mind then becomes territorial, marking our speech with particular emphasis or vocalization. Words that convey the feeling of "oh dear," that everything is just too difficult to manage, and that movement forward seems impossible may be those of the vegetative self, where the mind is dominated by our feelings. If our words reflect old models, beliefs, and the sense that things are etched in stone or are black and white, with little room for varia-tion, we may be speaking from our material self. This is when we become narrow minded, as is often the case when the force of our origins remains paramount. A word or sentence tinged with sarcasm, implied history, or a hidden agenda will cut as deeply as any sword. An inappropriate word may throw people into reac-tion as it touches an old hurt or grievance.

When we refer to someone as "inhuman," a "low-life" or a "predator," we are actually pointing to the force that is in charge at that moment.

When we communicate, our language contains the force of our ideas, musings, history, and erudition, which can either elicit a positive or negative response. We sometimes use language to manipulate an outcome. A lawyer may use "legalese" to obscure the reality of events or to sway the jury in a particular direction; the decision by the media of how to impart information to the public can color our perception of our communities, countries, and the world; we can be "sweet talked" by the seductive language of someone who wants something from us. Diplomacy is a cultural art form developed to counter this tendency to misinter-pret language. Language then becomes a tool to create peace or understanding. It strives to bring together all parties to find and touch their common humanity.

"O Prophet of God, which is the greater war?" He replied, "Struggle against the lower self."
—The Qu'ran

Language is but one aspect of human culture, within which there are myriad sub-cultures. These various subcultures may touch, connect, enrich, and inspire one person, yet affect another in a completely different way. It is through our culture that we express ourselves, communicate our thoughts, and share our ideas, writ-ings, songs, music, art, dance, and traditions. When human culture carries within it the nuance of the Great Life, it elevates the human self and society as a whole. As we express ourselves with Grace, humankind will pass on a legacy of inclusiveness, love, and a common higher purpose.

On a visit to Tuscany in Italy, Solihin and I went early one morning to Sant' Antimo, a very old Benedictine church and monastery. On entering the beautifully simple stone church, we were immediately struck by the sound of Benedictine prayers being sung. At first we wondered if it was a recording. Then we caught sight of a man who stood in one of the alcoves off to the side. He sang the prayers with such feeling and simplicity that we and the few other people in the church all became very quiet. Solihin and I sat in a pew, listening and watching the early morning sun streaming in through the window and illuminating the ancient stone floor.

As we sat in this place where people have worshipped for hundreds of years, I felt a deep internal response. Although the prayers were Christian, they sounded universal. It reminded me of Jewish prayers, of Islamic prayers, of spontaneous songs of worship that I have witnessed. I feel that we experienced the content of worship of God, regardless of the outer form of how it was expressed.

When he finished, the man gathered up his music, slung his leather bag over his shoulder, and quietly left the church. Just then, the huge wooden doors opened, and a busload of Italian matrons came clattering into the church, leaving far behind the exquisite moments that we had just witnessed.—Alicia

Religious training and practice provide a foundation and framework through which to understand our connection to the Great Life and our spiritual experiences. Reflecting upon these experiences and on our lives can develop an inner wisdom that enables us to differentiate between the presence of Grace and those forces that merely alter our perceptions and feelings. In our busy lives we may seek spiritual enlightenment or transformation through techniques that promise immediate release or salvation. Our animal self clamors for instant gratification, even in the world of spirit. With patience, however, we begin to see that the action of Grace and the workings of the mysterious cannot be hurried.

Religion is to me an expression, innate within the human, through which we revere and acknowledge the mystery of Life, with the hope that

this mystery will also guide us. It is a path or way that serves to guide me towards my destiny, giving me a set of references, rules, rituals, and legacies. It is collective, as many people belong to it, thus giving me a sense of a tribe that is more encompassing and human, as it transcends color and race. Its animal force creates territory, sometimes placing boundaries between us and others. Religion provides a foundation that animates and nourishes our feelings, and, while placing us into a tribe, admonishes us to look beyond with inspiration and hope.

Although I am a Muslim, my own particular genetic stock does not carry the nuance of eastern philosophies. I can nevertheless attest that over the years I have developed within me an appreciation, recognition, and acknowledgement of the many expressions of worship that I contain. I can sense and appreciate the pagan–reverent of the world as a living system and of our ancestors as those who paved the way. I can sense the Hindu in me when I begin to open my heart and my eyes and see God in everything. I can taste the Tao as the philosopher within who travels the path towards a wide and noble humanity. I realize that God is within, and that the seed of inner knowing and outer learning brought by Judaism lives in me, too. As I have slowly opened my hurting, closed heart I have opened too my inner heart that beats with the love of the Creator and of the Christ. I am ready to fight the jihad within, to overcome the petty thief within me that usurps my self and allows ego, will, and emotions to wreak havoc with my life. Like Ala'din, I must learn to polish my vessel and understand the unseen forces that both help and thwart me. I am one, and I become so by acknowledging the One both within me and without. In so doing, my forces bow down to the One, as they, too, are servants.—Solihin

Like the bees gathering honey from different flowers, the wise accept the essence of different scriptures and see only the good in all religions.
—Hinduism

Seeing one another in an open, wide, and nonjudgmental way is a prerequisite for human life. Most of us see ourselves both as individuals and as members of a nation or country. We see each other individually and nationally in various ways that are colored by our own views, history, and feelings. Every country has a psychic element—its own collective national consciousness. This collective psyche may also contain hidden negative elements that sometimes shadow a nation. The force of these shadows is most apparent when times are difficult—when we feel threatened and operate in survival mode. If we allow the force of a collective psyche to shadow our own reflective thought, we may fall into the duality of "us versus them," "we're right and they're wrong," or, "we're good and they're evil." It is much easier for us to see the shadow in others than in ourselves—whether locally or globally. When our viewpoint becomes polarized and we see others in terms of "them and us," we lose sight of our common humanity.

To him in whom love dwells, the whole world is but one family.
—*Buddha*

Our ancestors were members of large extended families who lived in the same communities for generations. Because of this, most of us are genetically coded to remain in one place, close to home, family, and what is known and familiar. We may feel a nostalgia for the days when life was simpler—when everyone knew each other and their place within the community, which gave them a sense of belonging.

Over the last fifty years, we have taken a quantum leap forward in technology and communication. Now, as never before, we are exposed to information and opportunities to experience places and cultures that were unknown to our ancestors. We can no longer ignore the fact that times have changed and the world is in transition, which has catapulted us into a new paradigm. We are being asked to expand our maps beyond the bounds of our predecessors, and this may be challenging as our coding may not contain the instructions on how to do that. We now have the opportunity to reframe and broaden how we see others and ourselves as members of a world community. When we value all human life and recognize its enormous diversity of culture, expression, and traditions, we create an incredible richness upon which humanity can draw. Are we willing to accept the challenge to move into new and uncharted territory?

As we begin to recognize the forces that operate within us, we realize how our mind is affected by the force of what it contains. In this way, our ancestry subtly affects how we think, our feelings engender a width of thought that contains the nuance of how we feel, and we carry an instinctual tendency to preserve old maps, territorial aspirations, group affiliations, and nationalistic ideals and to operate from a tribal consciousness. Similarly, our human mind may be adept at obscuring, obfuscating, separating, and being divisive. When we are mindful that we can see things only through our own eyes, and that our view of things may be jaundiced, or that we listen with ears that still hear the same old refrain, then we will see how these forces alter our essential humanity. Our mindfulness then becomes a tool to understand both others and ourselves, and to recognize that we are all affected by these unseen elements all the time. This predisposes us to move towards an ennobled state of consciousness, from which a new perspective on humanity emerges that engenders and supports life in a more global context, even if our contributions reside on a much more local level. Such an understanding helps us to develop a compassionate heart that is more open and less judgmental.

From our compassion arises the human quality of forgiveness, which creates a real possibility for transformation. Forgiveness and reconciliation free us from feelings of bitterness that can tarnish our relationships and eat away at the core of who we are. Instead, they bring us to a place of healing, lightness, and freedom from the weight of the wounds that we have carried. It is not only difficult to forgive others, but it is also difficult to forgive ourselves. We first must face and reconcile our own feelings, attitudes, and judgments that may obstruct the path to forgiveness.

Through surrender we can offer up old hurts, pain, and disappointments and create a space for the possibility of something new that is untainted by the past. As we begin to incorporate surrender into our lives, and at the same time are open only to the Source of All, we can move through life without being pushed or pulled off our path. But we must learn to recognize the times when we are led astray, initiate an indiscretion, or fall low, so that we can face our state and our forces. When we rise up again to continue to do our best, reflective about the forces that have influenced us, we polish the facets of who we are. If we allow what is hidden within us—whether good or bad—to manifest, then we can rise to meet the challenge to address and clean things that affect our feelings, actions, and essential humanity. This is the path of the human being, for whom the journey is as important as the destination.

Life offers us the choice of two pathways—one ruled by fate, the other guided by destiny. In the context of human life, these two words have very different meanings. Fate is the consequence of being controlled by the lower forces, not unlike a ship without a rudder on the open sea whose course is at the mercy of the prevailing wind and current. Destiny relates to the discovery and realization of our inner purpose in life by making the choice to be guided by the inner

You yourself may already be aware of this broad meaning of "humane." Its foundation is a family feeling towards everybody, the feeling that humanity is one: one in heart, one in soul and one in worship.
—Muhammad Subuh

Self rather than the lower forces. With the support of these forces—whether material, vegetative, animal, or human—we begin the momentum towards a life guided by the Creator. This is the power that lies at the heart of one's true destiny, the source of which is higher than the human self.

13

The Inner Heart

Within every human is a vessel,
the container of our essence or soul.
It carries the Light within us and
through life and worship
it is cleaned and widened as our essence grows.
Our vessel is the container of the inner heart.
It is where love resides, where heaven and earth meet within us.
The love of the inner heart may remain here,
or we can envelop our world with it,
bringing forth change in our
families, friends, communities, and ourselves.

From below upwards:
Heart of earth [material]
Heart of water [vegetative]
Heart of air [animal]
Heart of fire [human]
Heart of Love [noble]

The heart in its most basic form is an essential organ built from the genome of our forebears. We may have a heart of spirit and courage or one that is wounded and vulnerable; one that is open and loving, or more closed and stoical; a robust heart, or one that carries the shadow of disease. The qualities of the heart that we inherit from our ancestors become a part of our own constitution.

Many religious and spiritual traditions use the heart as a symbol of love, embracing the idea that it is love that is the center and the expression of the One, and that through it everything can change. Although most cultures probably view the heart and love as synonymous, some are more expressive, and others are more reserved in their displays of love and emotion.

We all wish that the saying "love makes the world go 'round" were more evident in our lives. Unfortunately, most of us are more aware of the opposite—a world in which love is often not visible in our relationships, our actions, or our speech. Global terrorism has forced us—or perhaps given us the opportunity—to look into our hearts and see the world in a completely different light. Hopefully, this will bring alive a more global consciousness, and a more compassionate sense of the whole, highlighting our similarities instead of our differences. Although we may express our love in different ways, the blood of every human heart is red, a reminder of our common humanity and our common Creator.

Sociologists describe different types of love, which parallel our model of the life forces. They speak of logical, emotional, romantic, companionate, and selfless love, which are similar to material, vegetative, animal, human, and noble love.

The material heart is made of flesh and blood and what we have inherited. It can get sick, be lazy, be irregular in rhythm, become enlarged, or even burst. We call this material heart the *heart of earth*. This implies that our love is tinged by all our memories, and that everything we experience leaves a "footprint," just as the feet of the astronauts on the moon leave a mark or impression. This is a vulnerable heart, a heart that will play out our familial illnesses. This heart operates from a wound, remembering every hurt, pain, insult, barb, or rejection. Everything that leaves an impression acts as a force that sullies our love.

Throughout our lives and as we grow in our relationships, however, our hearts are tempered and washed by the feelings of emotional love. This is the *heart of water*. Even though this heart stirs and becomes unsettled, just as a pond ripples when a stone is thrown, it eventually calms down and again becomes still. This heart begins to wash itself, to clean its memories and become more adaptable and less hurt by the past.

For many of us, the hearts of earth and water are predominant. When we are patient and courageous, however, our heart becomes lighter and more pliable. Just as the wind blows through the willows and reeds, this animal heart is only momentarily ruffled by insults or ill-spoken words, allowing them to pass through. This *heart of air* is more placid and calm, yet it dances in rhythm to the force of carnal romantic love. It can be seduced by "greener grass," and it often takes things very lightly and casually. It may appear callous or unfeeling, but when accompanied by the hearts of earth and water, the heart of air is able to be light when things of the world might otherwise challenge our love.

Our human heart burns with fire, passion, and love. Its temperament inflames, and thus its heat and sparks are easily transmitted to others, who also become impassioned. The human heart kindles human love that is national or global, and thus inspires similar sentiments in others. This *heart of fire* is able to burn up insults and potential wounds. With our partner we may have a love that is tempestuous, fiery, enthusiastic, and intense. A heart of earth can smother another's flame; a heart of water will temper a heart of fire; a heart of air will ignite it.

In Islamic theology, the inner heart is known as the **qutub,** *or central axis, through which Love enters the world. Only when our mind is truly quiet can this Love enter and fill our vessel.*

These four hearts illustrate our inner development as human beings. Over our lives they may grow, or we can become held in our genetic code, unable to move beyond our familial patterns. We might vacillate between a heart full of memories and a heart that drowns us in our emotional turmoil. We can be blown from partner to partner, be too light in our relationships, or scorch another with our own fiery nature.

Being Human

Pray for a heart as wide as the ocean.

—Muhammad Subuh

As life shapes our heart it will one day contain all these aspects, each of which supports the growth of the inner heart. We can practice opening and widening our heart, and indeed pray for such a heart. If we are attentive of the different hearts, then our words and actions can be spoken from this inner place so that we are but the hand of God extended through our being. This is the *heart of love*, which allows the Creator's love to pour through us. We are then shaped by love.

14
Surrender

the sun leaves
yet dawn greets
plants rise to the call
animals follow the rhythm
humans surrender
nobility bows
and Life begins

The One conducts us, and thus orchestrates our various natures to work as a whole. We each dance to the tune of the Creator in our own way, yet some of us turn away from this music. Surrender allows us to reconnect. What matters is that we make the intent to face the Great Life. In our own lives we might move from one path to another, looking for one that fits. Despite being swayed by the forces, we hear the call of God, and gradually, if we persevere, we can be guided to the path of the One. That this path is different in its form throughout all cultures does not matter, for the content is the same.

In surrender, which holds within it the other essential qualities of integrity, flexibility and reflectiveness, we may be illuminated, brought alive, and made whole. In this quiet yet active state of openness, and with trust, faith, patience, and humility, we can be given an inner understanding of our needs or present situation. As we learn how to live a parallel inner and outer life, engaged with the world and yet surrendered to the Great Life, we are accompanied by an ever more present sense of our selves as human beings.

Last winter I had been struggling with a personal issue for a day or so, and felt unable to rise out of the dark feeling. One morning, I left home and drove through a thick fog. I could hardly see, and everything was tinged with gray. As I drove further up the hill, I saw that the sky behind the fog was actually blue and that the sun was shining. I had simply been unable to see it at the bottom of the valley. The fog suddenly cleared, revealing a crisp, sunny, blue-skied day. As I saw and felt the sun, my mood suddenly lifted. I recognized the sun as a metaphor for the Light, which is always there—it just gets occluded by our "stuff," which blocks it out. This was a reminder to me of how I allow difficulties to fill my awareness and become overwhelmed, burdened, and in the dark. When I remember to surrender and reconnect with the Light, I see from a more illuminated place, beyond the dark shadows into the possibilities that lie ahead.—Alicia

The word surrender comes from the old French, which means to "render up," "submit to another," "give back," or "yield." These meanings may be overlooked, and the word surrender may instead be seen as representing defeat, being conquered, beaten, or ruled upon, or foregoing our liberty. For example, several years ago we asked participants in a workshop to surrender during an exercise. One of them was a Jewish woman who quickly replied, "Surrender? The only reason that my people are still alive is because we have refused to surrender!" Similarly, in our Austrian workshops, some people have had difficulty accepting the idea of surrender, because Austria was forced to surrender in both world wars. The word immediately conjured up images of defeat, postwar poverty, and the loss of national pride. Sometimes we have the mistaken belief that when we surrender we have to give up, or lose a part of ourself, that we will be in some way diminished. A recent workshop participant said that she was surprised by how empowered she felt by surrendering to the Great Life.

To surrender, we need only do our best to make a space to be guided by God from within rather than be directed by outside forces. There are no words involved in the process; we simply present our self to the Creator. This silencing of desire, want, or need creates a place of stillness within that opens a space for the Divine. It is the willingness to let go, to offer up, to ask to be shown, and to make a space for the unexpected, free from any anticipation of the outcome.

In the holy books it is said that the way that leads to the completeness of life is not a path that can be made up, explored or planned by human beings—only by Almighty God. Human beings are required only to surrender; to surrender with acceptance and a willingness to let go.

—Muhammad Subuh

Our eldest daughter, Sofiah, is a dancer who went to India as a result of a strong inner feeling to study Indian temple dancing. She traveled around the north and found a school in Orissa that taught that form of dance. When she started classes, she found it very difficult to train her body to move in a completely different way. She was also disturbed by some of the seemingly harsh methods used to teach this very structured form of dance, which can take many years to learn.

Sofiah wanted to understand why she had felt so guided to go to learn this form of dance, yet was finding it so difficult. Each day she surrendered and asked to be shown what she needed to see. One day during her surrender, she experienced that she had devotional dance within her; that whenever she danced she expressed the content of her devotion to the Divine, and that it wasn't necessary to learn a particular dance form in order to do that. It seemed, however, that she needed to have this experience to understand this. She was then able to leave the school and continue on her travels through India. She is now beginning to teach others how to connect with their own inner, or devotional, dance.—Alicia

Muslim: *the Arabic word for one who is surrendered to the will of God.*

Although they are not the same, prayer parallels surrender in many ways. Prayer also comes from the recognition of something beyond ourselves that can support or guide us. It is a means to experience the transcendent and a pathway for us to render up our infallibilities and idiosyncrasies, to voice our disquiet and needs. People pray for many reasons, some as part of a ritual or a petition for assistance, and some on behalf of others. In every religion prayer is used as means to become quiet and present, and to connect with the Divine. Surrender can be incorporated into prayer by simply ending one's inner dialogue with a period of complete quiet, stillness, and openness.

Surrender is invaluable whenever one of our forces takes power or we feel affected by some external force. When we surrender to the Great Life, all the other forces align themselves to the One. Sometimes this will result in a change of feeling sufficient to move us out of our state, while other times it may give us the ability to see what to do. Its effect, not only on us, but also on those around us, can be quite remarkable.

Recently my sister-in-law Martha and I visited Connecticut for the weekend. On the morning of her departure, I accidentally drove past the airport exit, and we arrived late only to find a huge line. Stepping around the crowd, we approached an agent and explained the situation. He told Martha to go directly to her gate, and for me to wait in line with her bag, that he would put it on the next flight. We said our hurried good-byes, and off we went in different directions.

After forty minutes in line, I finally approached the counter. Unfortunately, the nice man who had promised to assist me was nowhere in sight. Instead, the agent who replaced him steadfastly refused to put a bag on a plane "without a ticketed passenger to match." Frustrated, I began to argue my point, but the woman wouldn't budge, adding, "This is so totally against the rules that I want no part of it." She then turned and walked away. In her momentary absence I got very quiet, surrendering the anger and frustration I often feel when things don't go as planned. I then realized that in the big picture, this was a rather small glitch, and I could work it out.

When the woman returned, I felt completely calm. I asked her if she needed to see some identification. To my astonishment, she replied, "Oh, no, this will be just fine!" Everything about her—her posture, tone, and facial expression—was different. Not only that, but she then accompanied me through the security check, chatting away as if we were long-lost friends. Her complete about-face surprised me until I suddenly recognized that I had done the same. My ability to step back and let go of my own stubborn posture had brought out the softer side of me as well. It was a clear demonstration that a simple act of surrender can dramatically alter our interactions with others in the most positive of ways.—Alexandra

*We are brought thick desserts,
and we rarely refuse them.
We worship devoutly when we
are with others.
Hours we sit, though we get
up quickly
after a few minutes, when we
pray alone.
We hurry down the gullet of
our wantings.
But these qualities can change,
as minerals in the ground rise
inside trees
and become tree, as a plant
faces an animal
and enters the animal, so a
human can put down the heavy
body baggage and be light.*

—Jelaluddin Rumi

The human mind is the great demon in the process of surrender. Different traditions use different ways to still and quiet the mind to enable a state of emptiness to occur. For example, meditation is one technique used to silence the mind. In the calm pool of emptiness, the call from the Great Life can then be heard. Some meditations employ primary sounds to instill a resonance within the self that enables us to tune into the primary frequency; guided or visual meditations create new pathways by taking the mind in a particular direction. Each of these models attempts to move away from the limitations of our normal reality.

Some people may attempt to use hallucinogens to facilitate a transformative experience, not realizing that each life force is unable to elevate beyond its own level. Thus, marijuana, opium, ayahuasca, or any plant-based hallucinogen will only catalyze its own vegetative nature. Although time changes, sensations are altered, and we become seduced into a new visual world, these hallucinogenic states are simply magnifications of our own vegetative nature.

Most religious forms create ritual to quiet and prepare the mind to be receptive to the Great Life. Song, prayer, communal recitation, and other rituals bring the participants to the Holy by creating a sacred space. In Islam, the ablutions in preparation for prayer and the simplified postures performed during the prayers parallel some forms of classical yoga. In other spiritual practices, techniques that increase neural flexibility create altered states of consciousness. The physiological changes experienced in holotropic and Sufi breathing practices and yoga pranayama alter perception, opening the sensory body by fully oxygenating the brain.

Every person will find the right way towards God for himself, and what may be the right way for one may be completely wrong for another...you must become your own self and you must develop your inner self if you want to find the way to God. You must not follow or imitate someone else.
—Muhammad Subuh

There are many different forms of fasting used to diminish the power of the forces and "put our house in order." Some are merely as physiological cleaners and regenerators, while others are used as a means to attain a spiritual state. When we fast from food, we remove our fuel, the vegetative life force. By withdrawing our physical nourishment, we see and recognize not only our dependence on food, but also how undernourished our spirit may be. Our struggle to make it through a fast highlights the weakness of our spirit and its inability to sustain us when challenged. When the inner self is nourished and connected to the Great Life, the outer body can survive on surprisingly little external sustenance.

The intent within all religions is to help us face God. When we worship in a church or temple we face the altar; Native American traditions, which see the Creator in everything, acknowledge all four directions; in Islam, Muslims pray facing the direction of the holy city of Mecca. It is important to remember that our shrines, personal altars, icons, and statues all serve simply as outer reference points that remind us to continually inwardly orientate ourselves to the One.

Surrender either awakens or reinforces our inner knowing, the inner compass that orientates us towards the Great Life, and it tells us when we are off track or turned towards something else. Practice makes its presence more evident to us, and it cleans away anything that alters the needle's swing to true north. It turns our heart towards Divine love rather than towards the love for other things.

In surrender we open ourselves to the enveloping and penetrating forces of the One. These have different but complimentary actions. Many people have had the transcendent feeling of being part of the whole; that all the action, reaction, movement, and stillness around them is part of them, and they a part of it. In that moment they become unified, present, wide, expansive, and filled with love. This sense of wholeness and unity comes from the presence of the Holy

Spirit which is communicating and guiding us into a sense of the oneness of creation. The experience of the enveloping force of the One leaves a lingering taste and a reminder of a profound moment.

Within the force of the holy spirit exists the realm of angels. The presence of angels as intermediaries, luminescent beings, carriers of light and hope, and messengers to the One of our despairs, lamentations, and pleas, is universal. Some branches of Islamic theology recognize the presence of an angelic force that surrounds and envelops us as the *Ruh Kudus*. In the Talmud and rabbinical literature this same understanding of the emanation of God is known as the *Ruah ha-Qodesh* or *shekhinah*—the earthly presence of the Divine—and is seen as an all-pervading female force.

Conversely, the second aspect of the One is a direct, more penetrating force. Although longed for, this force is more feared because it induces irrevocable change. This mystical experience of transformative union with the One has occurred throughout mankind in moments where the lower forces are rendered powerless. Because these ordinary forces do not want to give up their sovereignty, we may instead turn towards Grace, the feminine aspect which envelops, rather than the direct, more masculine penetrating force.

Surrender is a bridge, for it connects us with the force of the noble human. This life force comes by itself—we can't claim it, seek it, or will its presence—but with remembrance of the One and surrender as our guide, we are gradually prepared within to live a truly human life.

Being Human

15

The Noble Self

This trusting self
nourished by the fruit of faith
finds righteous patience
a humble heart
as surrendered
we obey the Call

As we find our true path and open ourselves to the One, we introduce the possibility of being touched by the noble life force. This fifth life force is intermediary in that it accompanies, envelops, and guides us to a spiritual life and the presence of the Great Life. Our actions then reflect this Divine presence. This noble intent resides within each of us, irrespective of our position in society or our material wealth. We may live a very simple and self-contained life, or perhaps we are an inspiration to those around us. The noble human being is surrendered to God, has a wide and expansive consciousness, and speaks from the inner self.

Tears may roll down our cheeks as we read, hear, or see actions that we deem noble. They come not from sadness or pain, but from the recognition of an inner longing to touch this part of our self. This ignites the innate spark of our altruism, inspiration, and desire to serve humanity. Some people seek to connect with their nobility by volunteering or supporting charitable causes, or through their choice of profession. Some find philanthropy to be a righteous action for the rewards of their successful business, and a way to give back to society some of their gains.

All cultures recount stories of inspired deeds that illustrate exemplary human qualities as well as elements of altruism or nobility. The characters span the entire range of humanity—from wise and benevolent rulers and warriors to ordinary people, servants, and children. European fables and the legends of indigenous peoples even describe certain animals as possessing noble stature and qualities.

These teaching stories often detail the plight of people who are held in the dark, caught by the unseen, or manipulated by the trickery of the mind and instincts. Some chronicle the adventures of those who have accomplished heroic deeds. They portray the trickery, thievery, lust, war, magic, and superstition of the human journey as well as the noble actions of the righteous and wise. Common to all of them is the discovery of a nobility of spirit sufficient to triumph over external forces. Challenged by their shadows or unilluminated selves, the characters are prompted to access their hidden yet innate resources.

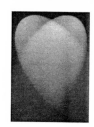

Hearing how others meet the challenges of their life's journey inspires us to do the same. Each of us is on our personal odyssey as we journey through life, the twists and turns of which provide an opportunity for us to find our many and varied resources. The willingness to face our challenges and see them through with trust, faith, and courage can take us in new directions, even when confronted by seeming adversity. An accident or unexpected event may be a wake-up call and an opportunity to be attentive, to question and to be reflective about why something has happened, and perhaps to see things in a new light.

The noble life force also has a relationship with our sense of identity. We inherit, borrow, adopt, and create many identities during our lives. While these form, shape, and enliven us, they may at times also restrict who we are. Our initial identity arises from our nationality—our soil, or the material essence of our origin. This is indicated when we say "I am American, English, Indian, Thai," and so forth. This has a powerful force for it brings with it the national sense of who we are.

There is a light in this world, a healing spirit more powerful than any darkness we may encounter. We sometimes lose sight of this force when there is suffering, too much pain. Then suddenly, the spirit will emerge through the lives of ordinary people who hear a call and answer in extraordinary ways.

—Mother Teresa

> *I was watching the film Rob Roy with Alicia. It is about Scottish intrigue, clan rivalries, deceit, and the battle against English oppression. The film enthralled me, for much of the story was already embedded in my own psyche through stories I had heard and read as a child, and through my own family history. The parallels in the movie struck deep chords within me. As the film ended I found myself in a completely altered state. Alicia turned to me, smiling, and said, "You want to be there don't you? I can almost see you wearing a kilt, with a dagger in your sock!" It was true. I could "feel" the coarse texture of a kilt on my thighs, which suddenly felt larger; different shoes shod my feet, and the hard outline of the dirk in my imaginary stocking was clearly evident. I could also sense a huge sword in my hands. As I sat there, full of the warrior, I suddenly became aware that I had always carried this Scottish archetype, and yet I had not fully understood or honored its noble qualities. Despite having the*

courage to fight my battles and go into difficult situations, I was often unduly confrontational and objectionable as a youth.

I also became aware that, inside me, my father's Scottish nature had resided side by side with my mother's "Englishness." The English and the Scots waged a silent yet continual battle within me. It made sense of the times that I had felt that Alicia's feminine will had dominated me, for this paralleled the historical reality of how the English once ruled the Scots. The hidden anger and distaste for their masters still ran through my veins.—Solihin

When a particular aspect of the vegetative, animal or human force takes precedence, we will derive our identity from the qualities associated with that force. For example, when we are ill or faced with unease or disabilities, our identity is shaped by how we feel. This disrupts the organization of the self, as our feeling nature becomes the focus of our identity: "I am sick / a recovering alcoholic / asthmatic / allergic/ in cancer recovery."

When we identify ourselves as an athlete, body builder, personal trainer, salesman, hunter, or by our sexual orientation, we then become identified with our animal nature or what we "do." When we derive our identity from our human self, erudition and knowledge become paramount, and education or profession defines who we are: "I am a Ph.D." / "doctor" / "lawyer" / "CEO." These are all examples of outer identities, the force of which may hold us in a niche or cause us to hold someone else to his or her perceived identity. We also employ systems that establish and reinforce a sense of hierarchy and order. The military, honorifics, and titles all demonstrate this through the use of rank. Rank is both recognition of the implicit order of the universe, and recognition of our position within a structured society. It implies that we know our place. We unconsciously judge, sort, place, and categorize each other. In this way we may superimpose an external identity upon what is real at the inner level.

Our inner identity is touched by the noble life force. Our identity is then no longer based solely on nationality, race, state, sexual orientation, physical appearance, education, knowledge, or profession. Our inner identity ennobles each part of us and acts to fully support us in everything we do. The higher qualities of our heritage, our ennobled and wide feelings, our actions derived by a higher calling, and our thoughts engendered by Grace all contribute to an identity of the true Self.

16
Value

Each of us longs to know that our presence
on this earth is meaningful.
As we awaken the qualities of
integrity, flexibility, reflectiveness, and surrender
at an inner level,
the gem in each of us becomes illuminated
so that we can see the value of being human.

We all carry inherited values that resonate deep within our material nature. These value systems—whether familial, cultural, or national—dictate, albeit sometimes subtly, not only *what* we value but *how* we value others and ourselves.

Several years ago in Rajasthan, I was asked to treat a woman who had been afflicted with asthma since childhood. As she came to me she was experiencing great difficulty breathing. As I worked with her, she even experienced a feeling of strangulation. We found that this lack of breath was somehow related to the time of her birth. As her mother and grandmother were nearby, we asked them to tell us about her delivery. Although initially reluctant, they slowly revealed their story. When the daughter was born, the lack of value attributed to girls in this part of India had raised within them the consideration of infanticide, even in this well-to-do Rajasthani family. Even today, this desert culture depends on males rather than on females, who are seen as expensive appendages because they require the accumulation of very scarce funds for their marital dowry. The force of this archetypal cultural pattern had remained around the woman, as her life contained the specter of death by dint of a gender that was not valued. The young woman then understood that her asthma was simply the result of the force of this long-hidden secret. The collective recognition of this by the family enabled her to release it whereupon her breathing changed.—Solihin

The idea that a mother could consider killing her own daughter is abhorrent to most of us. Without condoning the idea, however, we can have compassion for the situation in which these women found themselves due to old cultural dictates. We may judge one another according to our own value systems, but if we widen our consciousness to see beyond our own map, we then create the possibility of understanding how the values of others have been shaped.

Sometimes we derive our sense of value from the material world, buying possessions to try to assuage an internal sense of emptiness. Or we may compare ourselves to others, whether by performance, physical attributes, social standing, or some other means. When our own sense of value is lacking, we compensate for this by seeking validation and approval through sexual relationships, by caring for others, by doing good works—anything done to gain a sense of value from outside ourselves. If we do not recognize our value (our gem) from within, the quest for validation of our worth by outside sources will dominate our lives. What is missing is the sense of the jewel of who we are.

During the time that I had a practice in London, I was visited by a young boy who had been suffering from headaches. Before I began to treat him, his mother took me aside and quietly confided that the boy had been stealing from her purse, a matter of great concern to her.

As I worked with him, it became clear that he had actually "borrowed" the behavior of an animal, and that the tendency to do this was a familial pattern. When I asked him if he could imagine himself as an animal and what it might be, he replied, "a fox." I could see how the young man had used these clever, sly qualities to steal from his mother. It was evident that he had never really seen his own value as a human being and was therefore relegated to borrowing–in this case stealing–things of value.

I asked if he could explain what a gem was and its relationship to the concept of value. His answer was remarkably insightful; he responded that a gem was a symbol of something valued by society. I suggested that, before going to bed each night, he could ask God for a dream that would show him a sense of his own value. I was certain that if this were revealed to him, he would not feel the need to steal things of worth from others.

Several weeks later I saw him again. He grinned as he told me that his headaches had disappeared, and that he had had a dream where he was handed a red ruby. He recalled that he had actually "felt" the jewel in his hand. His mother quietly confided to me that he had stopped stealing, and that she had seen a remarkable change in him. His life was now guided by his new connection to his sense of value.—Solihin

A sense of our true worth is authenticated from within, from beyond our knowing. Through a connection to Self we begin to make our way through life on a journey that is guided by Grace, rather than governed by the forces of fate. On this odyssey we will meet our own "dragons" and face, battle, conquer, subdue, make peace with, and learn to dance with our shadows. We will be given the opportunity to see the value in our struggles, illnesses, darknesses and despair—despite the fact that during trying times it is probably the last thing we want to do. We can ask ourselves, What do I need to understand? What am I being shown? What can I learn from this? What is the gift in this? When we are able to see the value of all the parts of ourself, even those that lie within the shadows, we recognize the "gem" in what we have been given. As we live life with an open heart and see through non-judgmental eyes, we bring fully alive all of our resources, and we begin to know our purpose. When our lives have meaning, we start to sense our innate value.

No one person, culture, or nation is more valuable than any other. When we heed the call of the Great Life, it becomes clear that all of creation has value. We can then see all of humanity in one light; despite the myriad number of differences, our essence is the same. We are each a valuable member of the human family who seeks a relationship with the Divine. Now, more than ever, it is incumbent on each one of us to ask ourselves:

Do I see the value of the legacy that I have received from my ancestry, and how I can be supported by and use it in my life?

Do I stand tall, rising to meet the challenges of life by integrating all the parts of myself into a unified whole?

Do I act from feelings that are wide and inclusive and that bring me alive?
Do I see the value, richness, and diversity in the duality of life?

Do I have the courage, strength, and stamina to act for the good of the whole, fight for justice, and defend against that which is harmful to the planet, others, and myself?

Am I able to be reflective, to see something from the perspective of another?

Do I respect others' differences, and honor their humanity?

Am I willing to face myself and own my mistakes and shadows?

Do I have a compassionate heart and a willingness to forgive?

Do I do my best to surrender to the Great Life and allow myself to be guided?

As we surrender and bring alive our vessel—the container of our inner Self—
we begin to realize our own value as revealed to us through our connection to
the Great Life. Every aspect of our world then becomes a facet of the jewel of
creation. With a heart filled with gratitude for the opportunity to taste, breathe
in, and be sustained by all that life provides, our inner and outer lives become
one, and we begin to acknowledge the noble challenge of Being Human.

Epilogue

During the two years in which we were writing this book, there were many times when we got stuck, did not agree, or struggled with personal issues. When this happened, we would all stop what we were doing and surrender to come back to a place of quiet within ourselves. Doing this enabled us to put our own forces back in order and gain clarity about what we were faced with and how to move forward, whether collectively or individually. Each day before we began writing we would all surrender together as a way to prepare ourselves for the work ahead. We often surrendered many times during the day when we felt the need for guidance or clarity. If our opinions varied, or we were polarized in some way, surrender would enable us to articulate our differences from a more human place. Despite any challenges, our vision and purpose for the book remained clear. We learned to appreciate our differences and value the unique qualities that each one of us brought to this project. We laughed together, cried together, at times even shouted at each other when we felt unheard; but through all the ups and downs we felt the joy of working together, and were committed to doing so in a human way.

By this time you have probably begun to notice the interplay of the forces in your own life. As your awareness of them grows, so, too, will your understanding. We hope that this book enables you to see yourself, your relationships, and your purpose in life from a new perspective. Change is often slow and incremental, so be patient and trust in your own capacity to grow. By noticing and being aware and attentive of the forces in your life, you can begin to enlarge and widen your map, see things with new eyes, and face your fears knowing that you are not alone. Remember that surrender will not only provide guidance and put things back in order when they go awry, it also awaken your relationship with your inner self and reaffirm your connection with the Divine.

We would love to hear your stories. How have you used this in your life and what have you learned about yourself?
Please email us at alicia@adhumanitas.com to share your experiences.

with love,
Solihin, Alicia and Alexandra

About the Authors

Solihin Malim Thom

Solihin has always considered himself to be somewhat of a rebel, which perhaps can be attributed to his eclectic upbringing. At the age of two, his family moved to Cyprus and then to Kuwait, where they lived until he was eighteen. A brief spell in Beirut followed by boarding school in Scotland (which Solihin hated and completed with poor performance) fueled the nonconformist within him. His sense of being an outcast coupled with a hunger to know himself took him through a self-destructive stage from which he emerged as he made his own rites of passage while travelling through the Middle East, culminating in two years in Afghanistan. These pivotal years shaped him, as he pondered his feeling of emptiness and the apparent purposeless nature of life. Slowly his adventurous spirit found its mark, and he went to osteopathic school, studied homeopathy and acupuncture in the United Kingdom, and practiced physical medicine in London.

His travels in the early years prompted Solihin to seek a sense of purpose. This initially led him to look at the spiritual side of life, which brought him to Subud in 1973, and several years later he became a Muslim to help him have both ritual and faith in his outer life and endeavors. This combination of an inner and outer life profoundly changed him, and after several years as an osteopath, he realized that most of us, including himself, have little idea why we get ill or why we live substandard lives, even though materially we seem to fare well. A series of inner experiences gave him the body of knowledge that lies at the foundation of this book.

Solihin's unique ontological approach examines the root cause of why we get ill, become dysfunctional, fail in our relationships, or sabotage life. Initially working with Francois Reynolds, the unfolding of the model of the life forces became apparent. Eventually it became evident that their male partnership needed the feminine aspect to really come alive. In 1990, Solihin began to facilitate workshops with Alicia, which truly revealed the need for both male and female views and internal perspectives in order to understand the forces. This knowledge and experience has helped thousands of people over the years to understand their personal ontology and the reasons why they become ill, or why their life fails in some way. It has helped many reaffirm and re-establish their connection to the Great Life.

Alicia Thom

Alicia grew up in the English and Welsh countryside, which led to a deep appreciation for nature. The oldest of five children, she attended a Waldorf school, where she first began to realize the importance of community life. Her parents, an architect and a sculptor, had a strong religious foundation and yet sought something more, an inner experience, finding it in the spiritual association of Subud. When she was fifteen, her family moved to Indonesia which expanded her view of the world and its rich and diverse cultures, giving her a unique perspective on life. At seventeen, she chose to join Subud for herself and has followed her inner path through that practice of surrender ever since. Growing up with Christian roots and living in a Muslim country broadened her religious affiliations.

She studied design, organized and cooked for events, and had plenty of opportunity to develop her creative, practical, and personal skills as she and Solihin remodeled various houses and raised their four children. Later, she became interested in acquiring further tools to facilitate an understanding of ourselves as human beings, becoming a Master NLP practitioner in 1989. She has cofacilitated personal development workshops with Solihin since 1990, both internationally and in the U.S. Married since 1976, they moved to Oregon from England with their children in 1991 with the vision of introducing their work in this country.

Alicia's life experience and travel to many different countries has given her a deep appreciation for the diversity of human life and the beauty of the earth, bringing a unique perspective to her work. More recently, Alicia developed the Sacred Woman workshop where she offers an opportunity for women to explore, recognize, and connect with their innate qualities and resources. She loves to explore the world, discovering unique and special places and sharing that experience with others. She and Solihin continue to cofacilitate the Being Human series of workshops, sharing not only their work, but also their passion for life and all that it has to offer. They live with their family on the bank of a river south of Portland, in West Linn, Oregon.

Alexandra ter Horst

Alexandra ter Horst is a self-proclaimed "eclectic American." Born in the west, raised in the south, and educated the east, she has hop-scotched the US in recent years, living and working in Dallas, Denver, Houston, Atlanta, Los Angeles, and most recently the mountains of western North Carolina. Her fascination with human nature led to a degree in psychology from the University of Virginia in 1979. Armed with her diploma, she began an employment odyssey that ranged from radio advertising sales to recruiting for an IV catheter manufacturer to owning a dirt bike training business, all adventures that furthered her curiosity about why humans think, feel, and act as they do.

A descendent of several Presbyterian ministers, Alexandra was raised in a spiritual tradition where Sundays were marked by worship in a large church in Dallas. Despite this, she struggled with her own relationship to her faith throughout most of her early adult years, longing for some deeper sense of her connection to God.

It was not until 1995, when she attended a workshop facilitated by Solihin and Alicia Thom, that she was able to gain a totally new perspective. So inspired by the idea that, by understanding these forces, we begin to understand ourselves, others, and our life's purpose, she embarked on an intensive study of the Thoms' work, and joined their organization later that year. In 1996, she became a member of Subud, a world-wide spiritual organization that she feels has greatly expanded her ability to worship God beyond her Christian foundation. Since that time she has traveled to such diverse places as Indonesia, Morocco, India, and Europe in pursuit of a deeper appreciation of the common bond that exists between all human beings. She is currently vice president of SymPoint Communications, a public relations firm based in Asheville, North Carolina.

Further Resources

Ad Humanitas

Solihin and Alicia Thom are co-founders of Ad Humanitas—an organization dedicated to furthering humanity within each of us as members of one global human community. Since 1987 people of many different ages, nationalities, and from a variety of spiritual paths have greatly benefited from attending workshops that further their understanding of the action of the forces in their own lives.

The core and foundation of the work developed by Solihin and Alicia is an understanding of the life forces—those elements that exist within and around us that shape our lives—together with an acknowledgement of the presence of a primary Divine force. In addition to private consultations, they provide *The Being Human* series of personal growth and development workshops for individuals as well as the *Inner Natures Integration* practitioner training/workshops for those in the field of health care.

For more information visit their website or phone them at:

www.adhumanitas.com
800 304 4464 - 503 723 7900

Subud

Subud is a worldwide spiritual community of people who believe in the possibility of being in touch with one's true self and one's humanity through surrender to God. The name Subud is an acronym derived from the Sanskrit words: Susila Budhi Dharma, which together symbolize this possibility.

Subud embraces all religions, all races, and all cultures. It has no religious bias or preference and is not based on dogma or creed. The only teacher in Subud is one's own inner self. If religion can be compared with a vessel,

Subud can be compared with the water the vessel might contain—the inner content, but not the form.

What one experiences in Subud is an awakening of one's own inner self. This is received spontaneously in the spiritual exercise of Subud—known as the *latihan*—which has its origin in the Grace of Almighty God.

For more information visit www.subud.org

Permissions

The Order of the Forces

The Order of the Forces

Our human self can tune into and order life, fulfilling the notion that we are a self-organizing part of Creation. When the forces become disorganized it is difficult for us to truly connect with our life and purpose.

We use cards with icons that visually represent each of the different forces. Over the years we have observed repeatedly that our workshop participants have the ability to recognize when and how their own life forces are out of order. Through their understanding of the forces and their surrender, they also find that they contain the innate capacity to put things in order so that they are supported by all of their forces. Reading this book will begin a journey in which you, too, will be able to recognize how the order and relationship of the forces and the five essential qualities can become disorganized and what is needed to put them back in order.

By placing the cards in a particular order we can gain an understanding of what is occurring within us. Sometimes we know that the forces are out of order and at other times we cannot differentiate which force is where. We can arrange the cards to help us see what aspect of ourself has taken power, been misplaced, displaced, or become disordered.

If you work through this exercise and get a sense that your forces are out of order, you may wonder what you can do about it. After placing the cards, the first step is to reflect on what this particular order might mean to you and to recognize that it will be a consequence of many factors: family patterns, home and work life etc. Simply recognizing the need for order will have begun the process. Remember that integrity is the initial ordering force, and also our connection to ourself and the Divine, and we need its presence in order to bring everything back into alignment. If you get stuck, don't understand what the order you have chosen means, or don't know what to do next, you can always come back to a place of surrender during which you may receive a new perspective, understanding, feeling, or simply make the space for something new to arise.

At the back of this section is a page of cards. Cut them out and use them to represent the order of your own forces according to how you operate in a particular situation.

Instructions for using the cards

Begin with a moment of surrender—a place of stillness and quiet, free of want, need, desire or thinking. Take the five life forces cards and place the card representing the noble life force on a flat surface. Because this force remains constant, this card is your reference point, and it never changes position. Next, take the card that represents the human life force and place it where it "feels" right, in relation to the noble card. Without thinking about it too much, take each card and place it in the position that *feels* correct. Place them in a way that most accurately reflects the relationship between your material, vegetative, animal, and human forces.

On the following pages we have included several examples of the most common ways in which people (dis) order their forces. Using the cards will help you clarify what happens, what you tend to do and where you place these various attributes. Where, and in what order have you placed them? Did you place them all together, perhaps horizontally rather than vertically? Have you misplaced one, or more? Have you placed one or more separate from the others? After you have placed each of the life forces cards, compare what you have with the picture on the next page. Most people who do this exercise will place the cards in an order that is different from this illustration! When you place the cards, you are laying out your history at that moment, and your innate *knowing* helps you to place the cards in the order that appears important. This is merely a reflection at that moment of what needs to be expressed. Even if there is some confusion in the process, the act of being quiet, and surrendering, invites the unseen hand of Grace to guide the process. Often people will lay out the cards with great clarity. They know exactly where they should go. Sometimes they have remarkable insights and know that they don't want or like some aspect of themselves, placing it out of the picture.

If we place the cards in their hierarchical arrangement (without the cards representing the five essential qualities) it would look like this:

The *noble* self is the intermediary that guides us towards the One, and our purpose in life.

The *human* self takes authority over its subservient parts, and also has the choice to be supported from above, and thus seeks the intermediary life force that will guide us.

The *animal* self is fed by our feelings, which gives us the strength, stamina and power to survive, supporting the human self by carrying out our actions.

The *vegetative* self is supported by our foundation/soil and provides nourishment, sensory input and maintains the physiological homeostasis of our animal self.

The *material* self is our physical body, the foundation that supports us, and our genetic inheritance.

For most of us, when we place the cards in the order that "feels" correct they will not be in the same order as this picture. This indicates that the forces are out of order! On the following page we have given you three examples, which are simple variations, so that you can begin to understand what occurs when the forces are out of order.

1   2   3

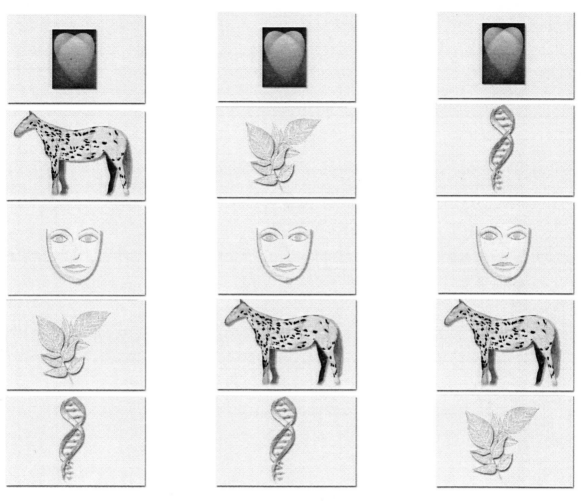

1. The force of our animal self has taken power—we are run by our habitual and instinctual behavior and tend to be reactive.

2. The force of our feelings dominates—we make choices based on our feelings and have difficulty in taking action as our animal self is also the wrong position.

3. The force of our familial patterns holds us to the past and may manifest inherited characteristics, habits and illnesses.

Being Human

1. When the human is displaced by the vegetative life force, the human self lives a life dictated by feelings; the prevailing emotion directs the action of the animal. Our human self is powerless and caught in a subservient place—static and passive because it in the position normally occupied by our feelings.

2. We are run by our instincts and drive, fed by empowered feelings because they are in the position normally occupied by the animal. Our human self is powerless and caught in a subservient place—static and passive because it in the position normally occupied by our feelings.

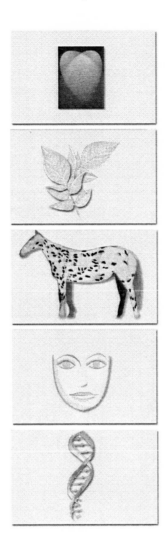

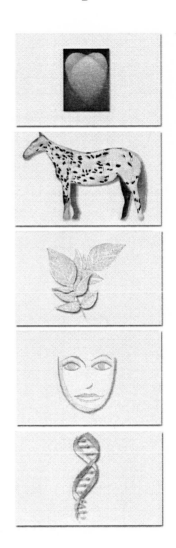

3. Separated from our material/ family/history our feelings drop down into our basement. This confines the feelings, making us feel neither alive nor receptive. Because our feelings have been displaced, we go through life unaware of the subconscious affect the material life force has on us. Our animal and human also drop into an undynamic state. The gap between human and noble indicates that we have lost our connection to a sense of nobility; a spiritual life seems distant.

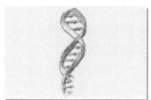

Being Human

Value (the gem) is a Divine gift; an inner sense of who we are.

Value

Surrender

Reflectiveness

Flexibility

Integrity

On this page is the normal arrangement of the elements of our self, including the relationship to the resources that give us the capacity to live a dynamic life. The five essential qualities of integrity, flexibility, reflectiveness, surrender, and value are not only an essential component of our outer life, but also the resources that awaken our inner life. Once you have arranged the life forces cards, take the remaining five (the essential human qualities) and place each one into your existing pictogram. You will do this by asking your self, "where is my integrity?" and "where is my flexibility?" etc. Or, "where do I place this quality." You may ask, "to what do I surrender?" Or "where I have I placed my value?" and position your cards accordingly. Once again, we have included some examples on the following pages to help you understand your arrangement of cards.

Surrender (the dove) is the bridge between the human and noble self, opening us to Grace, to be enveloped and penetrated, guided.

Reflectiveness (the eagle) is the bridge between our instinctive and human self, and brings illumination and vision, a new and wider perspective.

Flexibility (the snake) bridges our feelings and animal or instinctual self, bringing life, rhythm, transformation, and a width of consciousness.

Integrity (the staff) connects the material or historical self with the vegetative / feeling self, bringing order, wholeness, integration, and connection to our soil, ourself and God.

When we displace our integrity, our human house has less intrinsic strength, and we are unable to differentiate between our material and our feeling natures. This means we can no longer discern what arises from where. We lose connection with things, feel disjointed, can't pinpoint why, and are often "in the dark." We lack a sense of connection to the Creator.

Being Human

When we misplace our flexibility, we may not see its value or why it is needed. Our feelings and instincts merge, making it difficult to differentiate our feelings and emotions from reaction and drive. Because the snake is synonymous with our physiology, our animal self may not be appropriately nourished or adequately provided for. We will have altered cycles and disturbed function. Unable to rise out of our emotional state, we thus reflect life through our feelings.

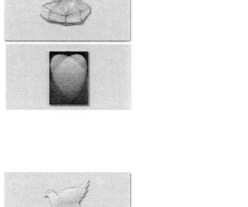

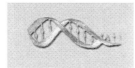

If we misplace reflectiveness, or perhaps have simply never recognized this part of ourself, then we operate merely from our instincts. This occurs when the mind "gallops off" down the wrong path, makes sweeping assumptions, or hastily defends itself from perceived attack. Reaction—rather than stepping back to consider the situation—is the modus operandi. We may be reflective but we are somewhat dissociated from it, and may simply think that our normal reactive and habitual thoughts are a form of reflection.

Being Human

When we put aside the need for, or sense, of surrender, we may rely on the mind for the answers rather than seeking guidance from a higher authority. Many people surrender to something else—their material self or possessions, their feelings or emotions, their power and habits, or their mind. If you have placed this card beside one of the life forces cards, it may indicate that you have surrendered or "bowed down" to that particular nature/force.

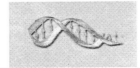

When we displace our integrity we have lost our connection at every level, and therefore cannot rise out of our material, as our feelings, actions, and thoughts are confined to the parameters of our genetic coding. With no integrity present for reflectiveness (the eagle) to roost upon, the mind can fly high, be tricky and clever, and mimic human values and erudition. Because the human is not connected to anything above it, everything is mediated through the human mind. When we displace our flexibility, we lack a width of consciousness, feeling, action, and thought. When we displace surrender, it may be because we have put it aside, do not see its importance, or feel no relationship with it; we are unable to be guided from within.

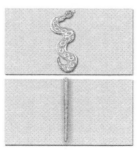

Being Human

In this example each of the five essential qualities is out of place. They are ungrounded and far removed from the human. Flexibility (the snake) is in the head so that the mind is always active and never still. In addition, value (the gem) has been placed on lofty ideas, trying to connect with, or pinpoint (integrity) the spiritual (the dove) with the reflective mind.

When we place flexibility and reflectiveness out of the picture there is no differentiation between the feelings (vegetative), instincts (animal) and thoughts (human). Despite the fact that integrity is present there is a narrowness or rigidity of thought because of the lack of flexibility. The mind becomes obsessive, but cannot sense or see it, so ultimately the reflective mind will tend to kill off aspects of life (flexibility), just as an eagle preys upon a snake.

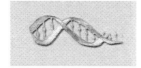

In this example the cards representing the human and animal are placed at the level of the material, indicating that these forces are held in the basement. The vegetative, integrity and flexibility cards are also placed where they are not useful to us, even though we may be aware of them. This means that each of those parts of us are governed by our genetic coding. We will be unilluminated, stuck, and held in our patterns, with no apparent way to get out. Our reflectiveness, our capacity to see what is going on, is far removed. Surrender has dropped down where it may become the prey of the eagle.

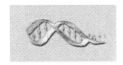

The Order of the Forces

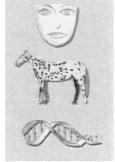

The vegetative, animal, and integrity have been placed in a horizontal arrangement in this picture. This infers that these forces and their corresponding qualities are comingled. Although they appear to serve us well, they probably do not in a time of crisis. In this example, integrity shares the same niche as the feelings and instincts. This may infer rigid or fundamental feelings from which one acts/reacts. Flexibility has been placed out of the way, indicating emotions and feelings that are not fully accessible, or addressed. This is often illustrated by those who fear snakes or see them as dangerous or representing evil. Surrender and the spiritual is valued, but there is no connection to it. Similarly, the ability to see or reflect on what is going on is limited.

Being Human

The Noble Life Force

Value

The human Life Force

Surrender

The animal Life Force

Reflectiveness

The vegetative Life Force

Flexibility

The material Life Force

Integrity

Being Human

is a Divine gift
an inner sense of who we are
or
placing value on other things

Value

Consciousness

The intermediary Noble Life Force
that guides us towards
worship of the One

Mindfulness

opens us to Grace -
to be enveloped
and penetrated, guided
or
surrendered to something else;
erudition, dominance, feelings, history

Surrender

The human life force
carries knowledge, culture,
beliefs, language, learning, philosophy
and religion and choice

Attentiveness

brings Illumination and vision,
a new perspective
or
allows our shadows, feelings, instincts and
mind to take 'flight'

Reflectiveness

The animal life force
carries our instincts, ambition, sexuality
power, habitual behavior,
the drive for survival,
defense and territoriality

Awareness

that brings life, rhythm, transformation
and width of consciousness
or
too active or passive
within an aspect of ourselves,
tricked by duality, too wide

Flexibility

The vegetative life force
carries adaptability,
receptivity, nourishment, addictive
behavior, healing,
our inner feelings, taste for life,
and awareness of the unseen

Notice

that brings order, wholeness
integration and connection to our soil,
our self and God
or
a loss of authority, order or misuse of power,
too narrow, rigid

Integrity

The material life force
carries our coding; racial, national,
familial and personal histories, creates
our physical foundation and
seeds our potential

TO ORDER

To order copies of this book, please contact Ad Humanitas Press:

800 304 4464 toll-free in USA
503 238 3273 from outside USA

contact:
alicia@adhumanitas.com

to order online:
www.beinghumanbook.com

Reviewers' comments

In the midst of rampant unethical behavior in business and government, pandemic drug use, social inequities and world-threatening violence Being Human offers clearly written, practical insights into how we may reclaim our heritage as noble human beings. It should be required reading for our time.

Reynold Feldman, author of Wisdom: Daily reflections for a new era

Being Human is a marvelous gift to all who want to live life more fully and with greater awareness.

Thom Hartmann, author, The Prophet's Praye

Being Human is a moving, insightful, and highly recommended contemplation of life's greater questions.

Midwest Book Review

Enlightening for those seeking a greater awareness of the forces that shape and influence the content of one's 'self,' this book is an insightful tool for re-establishing order and balance in life.

ForeWord Magazine

Being Human offers a coherent framework for understanding the hierarchy of life forces which underlie human potential for transformation. Integrity, flexibility, reflectiveness, surrender and value are each aligned with one of the life forces in this practical self-help guide. Honest, personal stories by each of the three authors are interspersed throughout the text, bringing a very "human" touch to Being Human.

Alternatives Magazine

The lovely quotes and poems add to the thought provoking and inspiring prose and anecdotes, making Being Human a comprehensive field guide to self-knowledge.

Marie Jones, author of *Looking for God in all the wrong places*

Some readers' comments:

"Being Human is beautifully and poetically written. It offers a model of the human condition that invites introspection and explains many of the factors which influence, challenge and motivate us. I found myself bookmarking many passages that spoke to specific issues in my own life and helped me to understand why I was struggling. Most importantly, this book has created a spiritual awakening within me and has strengthened my sense of connection to everyone on Earth, to generations past and to the heavens above."

"What a blessing this book is and will be as many of our brothers and sisters ... pick it up, purchase it and begin to uncover, discharge and reorganize their forces and claim ownership of themselves as a human ... graced and clothed with the Divine."

"Almost every night what I read seems to answer a question or an issue I am struggling over. So it is truly the best gift I have received this season! Never have I read such a convincing interpretation of what it means to be human. The simplicity of your language makes this powerful world view accessible to the general public while still challenging those who know its subtle complexities in the practice of daily life."

"The book is exquisitely written. The life forces pour out with every word. I don't want to read the book all at once. I want to savor, nibble, and really have the content and spirit of the book sink in."